BUILDING A NEW PERFORMANCE VISION

Break Down Organizational Silos and Create a Unified Approach to Human Performance Improvement

ASTD
Linking People, Learning & Performance

Thomas J. LaBonte

Foreword by James C. Robinson, Co-Editor, *Moving From Training to Performance*

Ordering information: Books published by ASTD can be ordered by calling 800.628.2783 or 703.683.8100, or via the Website at www.astd.org.

Library of Congress Catalog Card Number: 2001087856

ISBN: 1-56286-291-X

Contents

Foreword

"If we're so smart, why aren't we rich?" This is the question posed by Diane Gayeski and Anne-Marie Adams in their article "Barriers and Enablers to the Adoption of HPT" in the May/June 1999 issue of *Performance Improvement.* If human performance technologists (otherwise known as performance consultants and human performance improvement practitioners) are so knowledgeable about improving human performance, why are their clients reluctant to endorse performance improvement practices? Although "many training and HR professionals are convinced of the principles of HPT and feel confident in applying them," these professionals "are often unable to convince clients of the merits of this more complex-seeming approach." The authors conclude that "what we seem to lack is the ability to structure organizations so that people really want to improve performance—not just take quick action."

Building a New Performance Vision addresses this problem head-on. Tom LaBonte is an experienced and successful performance consultant who has managed both a learning and performance unit and an HR department. He has demonstrated the ability to

+ develop credibility with top management
+ address the larger performance issues
+ mobilize cross-functional teams to work on performance problems
+ implement multiple solutions that will improve workplace performance.

In chapters 1 and 2, Tom describes the underpinnings of human performance improvement. He develops a case study throughout the book to demonstrate that performance improvement cannot be achieved without management involvement because only they can change the work environment. He points out that some 80 percent of the barriers to performance improvement originate in the work environment rather than in individuals. Tom states that typical organizational structures encourage single solutions to problems. In other words, each support unit, such as training, HR, quality control, or IT, endorses and has expertise in only a *single* methodology.

Workplace performance problems, however, stem from *multiple* causes. Therefore, no individual unit can improve workplace performance by implementing a single solution. Tom thus builds a case for a *unified* HPI process that is endorsed by all support units. This theme of a unified HPI process is expanded throughout the book.

In addition, Tom stresses the need for a visionary HPI leader who can develop credibility with line management and has the strength to break down the functional "silos" that are barriers to a common HPI process. Here he addresses a problem that Jack Zenger described in an article, "The Invisible Wall," published in *Training & Development* in October 1997. Jack, who is a strong advocate of performance consulting, states that the problem "lies entirely within ourselves." Specifically, Jack concludes that we within the HR field are ". . . uncomfortable with some of the technologies of performance improvement, largely because we have not been involved enough in using it." He goes on to say, "We must begin experimenting outside traditional comfort zones. . . . As one who believes that you can change people's attitudes and beliefs best by changing their behavior, I think we must find ways to initiate new ways of behaving." Tom emphatically describes the need for a visionary and strong leader who can bring about this type of change. This leader must gain the support of both top management and those within the functional silos for a common vision and process.

Chapters 3 through 6 focus on how to obtain the support of the various units around the common vision and process. Using his personal experience, he describes how the HPI leader may either create a centralized HPI department or operate within a decentralized structure. The key is the ability of the HPI leader to articulate clearly how the various HPI units will work with management using the unified HPI process. Tom explains how to involve the various support units in creating an HPI process that all can support. This common process enables each unit to work in the same manner with all client organizations. Thus, no matter which unit the clients turn to, that unit will be using a validated performance improvement process.

Tom highlights the need to develop an internal network of individuals who are skillful and experienced in a variety of HPI techniques and solutions. This internal network along with external resources can then be mobilized to provide a wide variety of solutions, thus ensuring that multiple resources are available for resolving whatever problem is encountered. He describes how to develop the skills of individual HPI practitioners to identify root causes of performance problems and effectively implement solutions.

Chapters 7 through 9 show how to implement the HPI process. These chapters focus on the partnering with line managers and the importance of understanding the business goals and challenges. Tom describes how to identify specific performance problems or opportunities and how to contract with the line managers to work on those situations. The book includes an in-depth description of four major activities for utilizing, gathering, and assessing data and provides examples of data-collecting tools and instruments. In addition, it outlines how to facilitate a data-reporting meeting with clients, so that clients will endorse and support the solutions required to solve the performance problems. Tom also provides a comprehensive approach for selecting and implementing performance improvement interventions. He not only identifies the various roles regarding the implementation of interventions, but he offers a descriptive list of possible interventions for a variety of performance problems.

One of the highlights of *Building a New Performance Vision* is its approach to measuring (or, if you prefer, evaluating) the success of the performance improvement interventions. Tom advocates the use of the balance scorecard in chapter 10. Having used the scorecard in his own organization, Tom provides a compelling rationale for a scorecard that focuses on

+ client and employee satisfaction
+ financial impact
+ performance and process improvement
+ skills and knowledge improvement.

He provides examples of how the scorecard has been used by HPI units. He also describes the steps required to build and implement a measurement system based upon an HPI-focused scorecard.

This book provides the tools—worksheets and models—that HPI practitioners can use in their own organizations as they implement performance consulting. These job aids are based upon those that Tom himself used when he was in the role of an HPI leader.

I recommend reading *Building a New Performance Vision* because of the comprehensive and strategic approach that Tom advocates for overcoming the very common problem of organizations that are structured for quick fixes rather than substantial performance improvement efforts. Tom's experience in dealing with these problems in two organizations can provide performance consultants with additional strategies, tactics, and tools that they can apply immediately in their own organizations. Readers can certainly benefit from Tom's advice as they move toward their goal of creating a unified HPI vision.

Jim Robinson
Partners in Change

Preface

Bill, a sales manager, looks over his weekly sales report for the past month and isn't happy with what he finds. Overall sales per employee per week are targeted at 12.0. Between the first and second quarters, it dropped from 12.3 to 11.1. Mystery shopping goals on service quality include an overall score of 90 percent for each department. These scores declined from 91.5 percent to 88 percent in the second quarter. Customer satisfaction scores declined by nearly the same percentage as the shopping scores.

Bill is perplexed by these trends and continues to analyze the situation. Last quarter his team went through sales and service training. From what he could see, the training was well received by his department, but there is no evidence in his sales numbers of improvement in performance. Is something wrong with the training? Why didn't the training stick with the sales team? Does the business unit need refresher training already?

As Bill walks through his department he notices that a number of his sales associates are having difficulty jumping from screen to screen to finalize the sale. Is this a training problem or is it a systems issue? Did HR hire the wrong people? Whom do I call with these problems? Who has the expertise to help me get the right answers—and fast?

Susan, a division head in another organization is facing a different set of problems. Her division is expected to provide 40 percent of the organization's profitability. Lackluster business results and customer profitability data for the first quarter indicate that her division is barely covering expenses. The CEO meets with Susan and emphasizes that achieving shareholder and analyst expectations is a corporate priority. The organization's overall profitability requires a 60 percent increase in the net margin of her division by the year's end. Susan is given the charge to make it happen.

Susan is a strong business manager. She has 10 years of technical experience in her business unit. She has the reputation of being a successful manager. Nevertheless, in this situation, the way she has been achieving success and managing the division is no longer working. Susan recognizes that to increase profitability she needs to successfully change the business model of her division. She has no formal experience as a change manager.

Susan must lead her division through a major change away from a transactional approach toward a sales and customer service orientation. This may involve changing employee selection, new job descriptions, and revised training. It may also lead to creating sales and service incentives, setting up communication plans with employees and customers, and building new success measures. This change management process requires a fundamental shift in business strategy and a complete shift in the performance expectations of Susan's team. There isn't a lot of time to show results. Susan is unsure about what she should do.

More and more managers like Bill and Susan are asking questions like these:

✦ Who owns the process and expertise to quickly help me?
✦ Who understands my business well enough to help me achieve results?
✦ How do I establish priorities on actions that will bring me solid results?
✦ Where can I get support for project management that I can count on?

If Bill and Susan try to get these questions answered from within their respective organizations, what help can they expect from the various human performance improvement (HPI) functions? They will probably find that each HPI function focuses on the piece of the client's problem that they know best. Human resources specialists focus on selection, orientation, employee relations, benefits, and compensation issues. The organization development (OD) specialists within HR go one step further and emphasize the change process, cultural integration, and the role of leadership, executive development, and succession planning. Training and development specialists readily respond to Bill and Susan's requests for more skill building through the development of additional product, sales, service, and systems training. Quality professionals talk to Bill and Susan about process improvement solutions to their business problems. Information technologists (IT) review the information systems, analyze the technology and operating environments. Knowledge management specialists look for opportunities to share best practices and knowledge within and between business units. They also provide external business intelligence to improve business results. Each HPI function is eager to jump in and help.

What is wrong with this picture? Bill and Susan, as do many clients, face these situations daily without relief and become frustrated and angry. Each asks, why should I waste my time calling five or six staff areas for help? Why must I be the one to pull these functions together? None of these staff areas has the complete answer to my problem.

Part of the problem may be that several HPI functions—HR, training, OD, quality, IT, or knowledge management—operate solely out of self-interest.

Each of these functions often appears more interested in promoting its own agenda and its own success by engaging in "turf wars" instead of focusing on the client's business and performance needs. Why do clients need any of them? Nobody is happy with the situation, especially the clients, as they watch these departments jockey for position and influence within the organization. Is it any wonder that clients view these functions merely as a part of overhead expense?

Is Bill or Susan's scenario far fetched? Unfortunately, the reality is that all too frequently their experiences are the norm instead of the exception. In many organizations, the HPI functions operate in "silos," consuming vast resources while offering little in the way of sustainable results. It takes the combined models, approaches, tools, and terminology of all of the HPI functions to improve performance for clients like Bill and Susan. What is needed is a unified approach to HPI that taps the resources of all these HPI functions and integrates their efforts seamlessly to build successful performance interventions for the client.

This book is designed to foster a climate of cooperation to help internal clients and the HPI practitioners work together to improve performance. What this book advocates is a convergence of performance improvement functions across the self-created silos that exist in most organizations. *Building a New Performance Vision* argues that HPI is not the exclusive domain of any one function within an organization. No single function can offer a comprehensive process or set of tools to improve performance systematically across an entire organization. Instead of arguing across functional silos, a company's various HPI functions can find ways to work together under a single, unified process. This may seem to be a radical concept, but adopting it is essential to the competitiveness of any business or organization.

On the other hand, practitioners from these functions often complain that they are not valued for what they know or what they can do. Instead of blaming line management for this misperception, perhaps it is time for HPI practitioners to *turn the focus on themselves.* Rather than expecting the client to change, why haven't practitioners in the various HPI functions taken the hint and examined how their professions operate? Why haven't HPI practitioners taken the initiative to embrace a common performance improvement process for integrating the HPI functions in a powerful partnership focused on the client's success?

You will come across the term *client* many times in this book. The client can be a business unit executive, product line manager, the senior vice president of sales, or the executive vice president of a line of business. The client is the "owner" of a business unit who ensures that on-the-job performance of work groups supports the goals of the business unit. The client has the authority to take actions required to improve the performance of individual performers in the business unit. These actions include the power to change the work environment including organizational systems, work processes, incentives, information systems, tools, and other resources.

A Road Map to Creating a Unified HPI Approach

The purpose of this book is to present at least a clear path, if not a detailed road map, to show you how to move your organization toward this unified HPI process. Woven throughout the book is the case study of Bill and Susan, the hypothetical managers introduced earlier. The case study will help you see how the concepts developed in *Building a New Performance Vision* can be applied to unify the models, tools, concepts, and terminology of the HR, training, OD, quality, IT, and knowledge management functions under one HPI umbrella. Although the road to success may seem long and littered with potholes, this book will give you the step-by-step assistance you need to negotiate the rough spots in the road.

This book provides help for your journey by beginning each of the three sections with a list of goals that you will need to accomplish before moving along in the process. Each chapter then includes action steps you can take to build a unified HPI department at your organization. At the end of each chapter, you will find a quick wrap-up and a set of key points to make sure you understand what you have learned and how this knowledge will take you to the next step in the process. This book does not seek to answer all your questions. If, however, you are considering such a transition, you will find plenty of help whether you serve as a leader or as a member of the support team for an HPI integration effort.

Appearing throughout the book are the following helpful icons that identify recurring features and will help you create a more memorable experience when using the text.

| Action Steps | Case Study | Progress Milestones | Key Points of This Chapter |

Who Should Read This Book?

This book is written primarily for the internal HPI manager and practitioners from a variety of performance improvement functions who are currently working as HPI professionals, namely

- ✦ quality and process improvement professionals
- ✦ OD specialists

+ training designers and facilitators
+ measurement and evaluation specialists
+ HR and training managers.

Building a New Performance Vision will also appeal to those who do not normally think they live under the umbrella of HPI. These professionals are vital to the success of implementing the integrated solutions presented in this book. They are

+ HR generalists and specialists
+ internal consultants
+ industrial psychologists
+ knowledge management specialists
+ information technologists
+ strategic planners.

In addition to internal practitioners moving to integrated HPI solutions, external partners or suppliers will also find this book a useful tool in working with organizations moving to a single process focus for improving performance.

Acknowledgments

In February 1994 I started a new position as the head of training for a large corporation. I needed to create a new process and a new organization and to help trainers make the transition into roles other than classroom facilitators. I also had the daunting challenge of establishing credibility with line managers for the new performance improvement and training department as a value-added function. Where to start? I remembered attending a session at a recent ASTD conference where the concept of performance consulting was presented. After a little digging, I found Jim Robinson's phone number, discovered he was a neighbor located over the next hill south of Pittsburgh, and called him in for a meeting. Over the next several years, we successfully implemented performance consulting with my team. This initial business engagement grew into a professional and personal relationship with Dana and Jim Robinson of Partners in Change. Dana and Jim are mentors and friends. Both generously spent their time reviewing the manuscript and providing recommendations that tremendously improved the focus and quality of this book.

I am blessed by the generosity of a few other individuals whom I am honored to call my friends. Their support and efforts helped me turn a rough concept into this book. Many thanks to Dick Handshaw and Ron Hagy for their many years of friendship, encouragement, and support for my work on this book.

I dedicate this book to the women in my life—Starann, my wife, and Heather and Jennifer, my daughters, Eva Mick Estes, my mother, Anne Hope Malcolm, my sister, Ruth Breit, my mother-in-law, and Verna Johnson Mormor—and to my brother John LaBonte. I gratefully acknowledge their support throughout this endeavor.

Tom LaBonte
May 2001

 **PART ONE**

What Is Human Performance Improvement and Who Are Its Practitioners?

art one of *Building a New Performance Vision* provides a brief background in HPI and sets you up to make some crucial, first-step decisions on the road to an integrated human performance improvement (HPI) process. Unfortunately, no definition of HPI is universally accepted. Each department uses different terms and definitions for performance improvement and defines it from the narrow perspective of its own silo. Chapter 1 ("What Is Performance Consulting?") provides some of the more prominent definitions and then suggests some definitions that may be used as a starting point for all HPI practitioners. This is an important first step to breaking down silos and building one HPI process.

Just as there is no common definition for HPI, there is no widely held concept on which functions have a stake in HPI. Chapter 1 also presents a broader concept on the inclusion of functions under the umbrella of HPI. A strong recommendation is presented that the participation of functions in HPI must be inclusive rather than exclusive for clients to receive complete performance support.

Chapter 2 ("Who Will Lead the Change?") will help you determine which competencies the new HPI department leader must have to be successful, including the role of change agent and leadership qualities needed to spearhead the effort. The practitioner as an individual change agent, influence leader of peers and clients, and potential consulting team leader is explored as a prerequisite for the integration of functions and transition to performance consulting.

Part one lays the foundation for creating a unified HPI approach for your organization. The goals for part one are the following:

1. Acquire and develop new performance consulting skills and knowledge.
2. Consider who might be an appropriate HPI leader to align process, organization, and practitioner readiness.
3. Think about how the organization can identify and rally around one HPI process. A unified HPI process provides the glue and serves as a road map to bring the various functions together.
4. Think about ways to get buy-in from other HPI practitioners. Their active participation and leadership are critical to the success of the new HPI department.
5. Find ways to sell the changes you are proposing to make in the organization.

What Is Performance Consulting?

Isn't performance consulting just another fad? When did performance improvement get its start, and what are its origins? Why are there so many terms in use today that relate to the field of performance improvement? What are human performance technology (HPT), performance consulting, process improvement, and HPI? Aren't these terms really referring to the same type of activity camouflaged in terms that are owned by different functions of the performance improvement profession?

The purpose of this book is not to solve the ongoing debate of terminology among advocates of performance consulting, HPT, process improvement, and HPI. Each of these terms is used in the marketplace and has merit.

Human performance improvement and *performance consulting* are used synonymously in this book. This book focuses on the need for building a common process, tools, and terminology that can be used by practitioners to reach consensus on how to support their clients. To do so requires an understanding of the early origins and concepts associated with performance improvement. The following action steps, which are covered in this chapter, will help you learn more about HPI's origins, terms, and concepts.

Action Steps to Acquire Knowledge of Performance Consulting

1. Determine the origins of human performance improvement.
2. Define human performance improvement.
3. Focus on identifying the clients and their business needs.
4. Avoid the outsourcing zone.
5. Apply your knowledge to a case study.

Action Step 1: Determine the Origins of Human Performance Improvement

Figure 1-1 presents a list of some significant contributors to the early founding and evolution of HPI. The accomplishments of these contributors and many other HPI professionals over the past half-century have built the models, tools, and concepts that are represented in the new HPI definition and process advocated in this book. In looking over the list of contributors, it is apparent that HPI enjoys a history that often goes unrecognized by new or existing practitioners. Human performance improvement is not a fad.

Three of these contributors—Skinner, Gilbert, and Rummler—deserve special mention for their special contribution to the early development and later growth of HPI. The roots of HPI are found in the early work of B.F. Skinner. Skinner, the founder of behavioral science, believed that the task of scientific analysis is to explain how the behavior of a person as a physical system is related to the conditions under which the individual lives. Behavior can best be influenced by rewarding a partial behavior or a random act that approaches the desired behavior, that is, through operant conditioning (Skinner, 1953). This link between an individual's behavior and the environment is one of the theoretical foundations of performance improvement.

Tom Gilbert established the principles of performance improvement used today by most performance consultants. He focused on the changes needed to help typical performers improve into exemplary performers. Gilbert identified six variables that are required to improve performance. These include three work environment variables (information, resources, and incentives) and three individual variables (knowledge, capacity, and motives). Gilbert emphasized that the absence of performance support in the work environment, and not the lack of knowledge and skill, is the single greatest barrier to achieving exemplary performance. He stressed that in improving performance it is necessary to focus on the work environment variables before addressing the individual variables (Gilbert, 1996).

Geary Rummler's writings provided a framework for implementing performance improvement through the alignment of three levels of performance. He advocated the need for analyzing and aligning the organizational processes he describes as "white spaces on the organizational chart" (Rummler & Brache, 1995). Rummler indicated that process, organization, and the readiness of performers must be aligned and implemented in parallel to sustain exemplary human performance. Change in just one level will not sustain improvement because each level influences the outcomes of the others (Rummler & Brache, 1995).

Skinner provided the early theoretical framework, Gilbert the focus on work environment, and Rummler the emphasis on alignment of process,

Figure 1-1. Selected contributors to HPI.

Contributor	Area	Description
Chris Argyris	Organization development (OD)	Developed concepts such as action science, senior management team building, and the learning organization to help practitioners close the gaps in the performance problems and issues that exist between individual performers and their organizations (Argyris, 1993)
W. Edwards Deming	Total quality management (TQM)	Developed principles of TQM in post–World War II Japan that led to breakthroughs in efficiency, productivity, and standards of excellence (Deming, 1988)
Joe Harless	Front-end analysis and instructional systems design	Performance interventions require front-end analysis (FEA) of the performer's system. The FEA data is used to build four types of interventions to improve performance: environment, selection, motivation, and knowledge (Harless, 1994)
Tom Gilbert	Human performance improvement	Identified six variables—three work-environment and three individual—that are required to improve performance (Gilbert, 1996)
Roger Kaufman	Strategic planning	Created a systems approach to strategic planning with three levels—society, organizational, and individual—used in solving performance problems (Kaufman, 1996)

(continued on page 6)

5

Figure 1-1. Selected contributors to HPI (continued).

Contributor	Area	Contribution
Bob Mager	Instructional objectives	Learning objectives are written as statements of measurable, expected performance, with conditions specified in order to improve performance (Mager & Pipe, 1997)
Dana & Jim Robinson	Performance consulting	Championed the movement away from training as a single-event solution to more comprehensive solutions offered by performance consulting and provided research on the role of the performance consultant (Robinson & Robinson, 1995, 1998)
B.F. Skinner	Behavioral science	Behavior is best influenced by rewarding acts that most closely approach the desired behavior. He developed the concept of operant conditioning (Skinner, 1953)
Geary Rummler	Three levels of performance improvement	Established the need for analyzing and aligning three levels of performance—process, organization, and job readiness—in order to create and sustain exemplary performance (Rummler & Brache, 1995)
David Ulrich	Human resources strategist	Advocated HR functions becoming strategic partners with line management, employee champions, and change agents for the execution of business strategies (Ulrich, 1998)

structure, and performer readiness, in creating a HPI capability for an organization. Practitioners need to examine the contributions of all of the individuals listed in figure 1-1 to gain knowledge and understand the purpose of the HPI functions in their organizations.

Action Step 2: Define Human Performance Improvement

For a profession that traces its roots back to the mid-twentieth century, the controversy over the usage and definition of terms to describe performance improvement seems curious. The reality is that there is no commonly held definition within the profession on the meaning of performance improvement. Depending on the book or article read, professional association joined, or conference attended, these terms can be defined with a variability that can be puzzling. The myriad definitions sometimes seem to indicate that HPT, HPI, process improvement, and performance consulting are

- ✦ forms of needs assessment
- ✦ methods to improve systems
- ✦ scientific, engineering approaches to improving results
- ✦ glorified forms of training design
- ✦ variations of OD and quality management
- ✦ business reengineering methods.

Often these terms are not defined at all, and readers or conference attendees are left to interpret them from the perspective of their performance functions. Within the profession and in organizations, this lack of clarity on the definition and purpose of HPI is a barrier to the performance functions working together. Another way of looking at this is that if the practitioners involved cannot with one voice define how they work together to support performance improvement, then how can they explain it to the satisfaction of their clients?

Figure 1-2 examines a small sample of the definitions used for the term, human performance technology, within the performance improvement profession. These definitions may be used as a starting point for each HPI function within an organization to reach consensus from the perspective of their tools, concepts, and process models. Identifying the common elements and unique factors about each of these definitions gives HPI practitioners from the various functions the background to begin building a common definition of HPI.

Each of these definitions has worked well for its respective owner. The purpose of examining these definitions is not to discount or advocate one at the expense of others. The opportunity lies in using each to build a definition of human performance improvement that practitioners can rally

Figure 1-2. Selected definitions of performance improvement.

**ASTD
(1992)**

"...a systematic approach to analyzing, improving and managing performance in the workplace through the use of appropriate and varied interventions"

**Harold Stolovich &
Erica Keeps
(1999)**

"...an engineering approach to attaining desired accomplishments from human performers. HP technologists are those who adopt a systems view of performance gaps, systematically analyze both gaps and systems, and design cost effective and cost-efficient interventions that are based on analysis of data, scientific knowledge, and documented precedents, in order to close these gaps in the most desirable manner."

**Joe Harless
(1994)**

"...a process of selection, analysis, design, development, implementation, and evaluation of programs to most cost effectively influence human behavior and accomplishment."

**Dana and Jim Robinson
(1998)**

"...is the science of improving human performance in the workplace through analysis and the design, selection, and implementation of appropriate interventions."

around in an organization as a starting point in mutually supporting the client. The definition must be as appealing and meaningful to those with backgrounds in training and instructional systems design as to those from HR, quality, OD, IT, and other HPI functions.

Several points must be considered in forming a common definition from the definitions presented in figure 1-2. From the standpoint of similarities, all of these definitions

+ emphasize analyzing root causes
+ include implementing interventions to improve performance
+ use language denoting the systematic approach to improving performance.

There are also subtle areas of difference that should be considered when creating a new definition of HPI:

+ Several of these definitions imply the need to partner with a client, the decision maker, or the leader of the business unit. None specifically includes the client relationship in the definition.
+ The concept of a comprehensive system of performance measures that are appropriate for interventions dealing with multiple solutions is not present in all definitions.
+ Practitioners from various HPI functions may identify differences in definitions that could become barriers to HPI cooperation based on the clarity, style, and practicality of using the definition within the organization.

In this book human performance improvement is defined as:

> *The process used to systematically partner with clients for purposes of identifying performance problems, analyzing root causes, selecting and designing actions, managing interventions in the workplace, measuring results, and continuously improving performance.*

What does this definition of HPI mean? Table 1-1 presents a breakdown of the concepts essential to understanding the implications of the new HPI definition.

How does this definition serve the purpose of a starting point for the various HPI functions in an organization working together? The HPI functions with an instructional systems design and training perspective are concerned that HPI be process driven in its approach, client focused, systematic in application, and that the HPI implement actions that derive from research and analysis. The HPI functions with a process and systems foundation (OD, quality, IT, process improvement) share the concerns of their ISD colleagues.

These practitioners also want an emphasis on the workplace and work environment issues, comprehensive measurement models, and a commitment to continuous improvement. This new definition is intended to provide enough common ground to enhance opportunities for mutual support and cooperation in breaking down the functional silos in HPI.

Action Step 3: Focus on Identifying the Clients and Their Business Needs

The definition of HPI presented in this book includes the client. Although table 1-1 presents a brief explanation on the meaning of the term, the concept of the client is too critical to HPI and the goals of this book to leave without further explanation. Who is the client? In this book, the client might be a business unit executive, product line manager, the senior vice president of

Table 1-1. Key concepts in the new definition of human performance improvement and their meanings.

HPI Key Concept	Meaning
Process	A series of steps or phases that serve as a blueprint for a consultant to identify actions that produce value for the client
Systematic	The process steps are organized and implemented in a methodical approach tested for soundness and consistency
Partner(ing)	A long-term relationship that transcends single events for mutual support between consultant and client in improving results
Client	The individual accountable for achieving the goals of an organization or business unit and with whom the performance consultant must partner to improve performance
Analyzing	Collecting and evaluating data on the root causes of a performance gap to develop objective actions for an HPI intervention
Interventions	Implementing actions derived from cause analysis that solve performance problems by integrating models, tools, and concepts from a variety of HPI functions
Workplace	The work environment where problems are identified and analyzed, actions determined, interventions implemented, and results measured for improved performance
Measuring improved performance	The use of an HPI scorecard of balanced measures that is used to determine the level of goal achievement against established standards
Continuously improving performance	The evolution of an intervention involving the ongoing cycle of partnering, reassessment, implementation of redesigned and new actions, and measurement to determine improved performance

sales, or the executive vice president of a line of business. The client is the owner of the business unit and is responsible for ensuring that on-the-job performance of work groups supports the business unit's goals. The client has the authority to take actions required to improve the performance of individual performers in the business unit. These actions include the power to change the work environment including organizational systems, work processes, incentives, information systems, tools and other resources.

It has already been noted that to be successful, HPI practitioners must develop close working relationships or partnerships with key clients and focus on their business needs. The emphasis on forming partnerships with clients and focusing on business results is fundamental to creating a successful unified HPI function and making the transition to performance consulting.

Action Step 4: Avoid the Outsourcing Zone

HPI practitioners, whether they are in HR training, quality, or IT, often react to clients' performance problems from a silo perspective. Regardless of the client's needs, they push their agenda, fail to communicate with other functions that can help the client, and offer single-event solutions for performance problems that really call for multiple interventions. In so doing, the various HPI practitioners push their function toward "the outsourcing zone."

The outsourcing zone is reached when HPI practitioners are slow to respond, reactive, and incapable of delivering effective, timely HPI interventions needed by their clients. As seen in figure 1-3, the outsourcing zone is the gap that results when the rate of change in the business unit outpaces the ability of the HPI department to support its business and performance needs. It refers to the downsizing or total elimination of HPI functions by clients who turn to external partners for performance support.

The outsourcing zone is a dangerous place for internal practitioners to operate within. Avoiding the outsourcing zone is a matter of getting all HPI functions to adopt one process to support the client's business and performance needs. Internal performance consultants have the advantage of being able to deliver integrated HPI interventions that address the root causes of performance problems. Remember, most performance problems are not the result of a single cause. A department that focuses only on one type of solution provides the organization with minimal improvement. Even if there is improvement, it will usually be of short duration. It is a hard reality for HPI practitioners and clients to accept that successfully closing performance gaps requires the support of all the HPI functions.

There are times even with the integrated support of the organization's HPI functions that clients will not receive complete solutions due to either

Figure 1-3. The outsourcing zone.

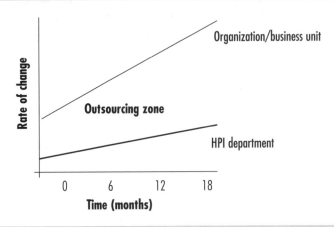

the complexity of the problem or lack of competency. In these cases, the HPI functions need the support of external partners. The new, unified HPI department advocated by this book needs the assistance of external partners or suppliers to supplement internal competencies and capabilities. Both external suppliers and internal practitioners need to work as partners for the good of the client.

Action Step 5: Apply Your Knowledge to a Case Study

The following case study shows why a single solution rarely is sufficient to repair a performance problem.

Management at a midsized service company had an employee turnover problem of nearly 45 percent per year among non-exempt employees. Although this high turnover rate was not unusual in the industry, management thought that their company's turnover was higher than their competitors'. Senior management wanted to know if this was a business issue that should be addressed or if it was just the cost of doing business.

The HR director understood management's concern and recognized that the constant churn of turnover was not only a barrier to improved performance for HR but also for the entire organization. The HR director volunteered to take the lead in pulling together a team to investigate the issues. The team consisted of HR staff, trainers, OD specialists, and specialists from the finance and marketing departments. They agreed to work together on a turnover pilot project with one job family, to gather some preliminary data, and to determine high-level causes of the retention problem.

The team determined from the data that turnover for the pilot group was at least 20 percent higher than their peer competitors'. An internal analysis conducted by finance calculated the annual cost of turnover at approximately $2 million. Data from employee exit questionnaires and from one-on-one interviews of existing employees indicated retention barriers in leadership skills and behaviors. The team presented its preliminary data to members of senior management. These managers agreed with the HR director's recommendation that a formal retention effort needed to be implemented, starting with the pilot group.

The team immediately encountered an unanticipated barrier to success. The business unit executive with responsibility for the pilot group with the highest turnover in the corporation did not take ownership of the problem. She indicated that the retention project would take too much time and divert the attention of employees away from production. The business unit executive recommended waiting until later in the year to start the retention project. The HR director and other key managers represented on the retention team decided to take the initiative and move forward with the intervention. The turnover problem was too important not to continue.

The retention team established a goal of reducing turnover in this job family by 10 percent before the year's end. The strategy was to demonstrate the effectiveness of performance consulting with an early win. This would, they hoped, pique the interest of the business unit executive, a key client, and galvanize participation in an HPI intervention for the rest of the unit.

For the rest of the year (9 months), the retention team worked on staffing models and on increasing the full-time employee ratio. Team members also worked on improving selection procedures, creating new and improved training programs, enhancing employee benefits, and working on compensation/incentive programs. As these changes were being implemented, there was a positive perception of their value by employees, the retention team, and management.

What were the formal, quantifiable results at the end of the retention consulting initiative? As the data was being collected to compare against the baseline, the expectation was that turnover was dramatically decreasing. When the data was analyzed and reported at the end of the year, the retention team was shocked and somewhat demoralized by what they found. Instead of decreasing, turnover for this job family actually increased from a baseline of 45 percent to 60 percent! The cost of turnover had increased to $2.8 million!

What is the moral to this story? Even when HPI practitioners from the various functions agree to work together on a common business issue and are taking actions that appear to be appropriate, it isn't enough. Without client involvement and ownership as a full partner in the intervention, the opportunity for realizing expected results is dramatically reduced. The client controls the business change process and the work environment. Performance improvement cannot occur without changing the work environment. Most performance consultants find that it is in the work environment where they find up to 80 percent of the barriers to improvement. Complete solutions to client's business needs are only possible when the consultant and client work as partners, implementing mutually supportive actions, success measures, and plans for improving performance.

Progress Milestones

This chapter provided a foundation in HPI to prevent confusion as you move through this book. Yes, HPI does have a long history that has encouraged ownership of various approaches. HPI practitioners must lay aside the history of competitiveness as well as ownership in cherished models and tools that provide clients with incomplete performance solutions. Practitioners must step out of their safe havens, their silos that they know so well, and become true business partners. One of the points of *Building a New Performance Vision* is that organizations today can no longer tolerate reactive approaches to business or "turf wars" among HPI functions for client ownership.

It will take strong leadership from within the organization to bring HPI practitioners to the table in building one process, one department, new roles and competencies. In the chapters that follow, you will learn how to provide leadership as a practitioner in influencing the effort to align competing HPI functions or become the HPI leader yourself.

Key Points of This Chapter

✔ No one definition of HPI exists. Find a definition that is comfortable for all your potential HPI partners and stick with it.
✔ When departments work at cross-purposes, often the wrong intervention is used to solve a performance problem. This is very good ammunition to use as you sell the concept of a unified HPI process to your organization.
✔ An integrated HPI process and department can help you avoid the outsourcing zone.

✔ It takes the combined models, concepts, tools, and competencies of all of the HPI functions in an organization to provide clients with complete solutions.

✔ The client must own the HPI process and be an active participant in a consulting intervention for the best results to be achieved by the HPI department.

ॐ **2**

Who Will Lead the Change?

The movement to a new, unified HPI process in your organization cannot happen without leadership. Some one, or some group of HPI practitioners, needs to call the question on taking the necessary steps to eliminate silos and the completion for client ownership. A visionary leader and practitioners with the willingness and ability to influence change are needed to make the transition to one integrated HPI process mutually supporting HPI functions that focus on client needs. You may use the following steps to develop a plan of leadership actions needed to integrate your HPI functions.

 Action Steps to Decide Who Will Lead the Unification Effort

1. Form an HPI leader selection team representing key internal clients, HPI practitioners and internal service partners. Create a selection plan.
2. Create a selection profile of the required competencies, experience, and behaviors to ensure the HPI leader's successful performance.
3. Identify practitioners willing to serve as change agents and advocates of the new HPI department and process.
4. Create an organizational and cultural integration plan for the HPI leader's first 90 days. Include an approach for gaining and maintaining CEO support for the change to a unified HPI process.
5. Identify performance expectations and early measures of success for the HPI leader.
6. Decide whether to seek candidates internally or externally and whether a search firm will be used.

Action Step 1: Form an HPI Leader Selection Team

Assuming that the HPI functions and senior management has decided to make the change to a common HPI process and structure, a leader with the experiences and competencies listed in table 2-1 is needed to make it happen. There are as many approaches to filling this position as there are organizations trying to find the right person. These approaches range from selecting a high-potential, junior member of senior management as a development opportunity, to doing an external search using headhunters. In many organizations, someone from within an HPI function is available and tapped for the job. Too often, the selection of an HPI leader is just another task to check off the to-do list; the result is that the organization hires someone whose qualifications are merely that he or she is priced right, available, and a known commodity. It is not surprising that such organizations are soon disappointed with the lack of progress that the new HPI leader has made in improving performance.

The leader selection team creates a selection plan with tasks and timelines assigned, meetings and progress reviews scheduled, and a communication plan outlined. An important component of this plan is the development of the selection profile, an essential first step in the process. The selection profile becomes the blueprint for attracting and retaining the right person with the right competencies and experience as the HPI leader.

Often selection teams start with preparing the formal job description. The performance expectations and requirements for the HPI leader differ for each organization. Appendix B provides an example of a generic job description for the HPI leader's position. This generic description can serve as a model for creating your own, customized job description for candidate HPI leaders.

When the selection profile is completed and approved by senior management, the selection team turns to its next set of questions. How is the HPI leader to be selected? What are the steps? Who must be involved? The team must recognize when answering such questions that it is not uncommon for the selection profile to generate candidates that could be described as mavericks. Successful change agents often operate on the outer fringe of political and bureaucratic acceptability. The very nature of their personality and approach to leading change may raise eyebrows among more traditional line managers.

Action Step 2: Create a Selection Profile of the Required Competencies, Experience, and Behaviors

The HPI leader serves two sets of stakeholders: clients and HPI practitioners. The HPI leader moves clients and HPI practitioners from the security and safety of their current mode of doing business to an unknown future. To do so, he or she must demonstrate the strength of character, leadership, and change management expertise to break down silos, create a new focus on client needs, and build a new department and HPI process. The role of HPI leader demands a proactive leader with the strategic insight to build consensus around a new process, create a unified HPI vision, and motivate all HPI practitioners to learn and apply new skills. The HPI leader serves as a champion of integrating HPI functions and a champion of the HPI process. Clients and practitioners have certain expectations of the HPI leader. These are outlined in table 2-1.

To be successful, the HPI leader must identify the core needs of clients and practitioners, find areas of common interest, and fulfill these expectations consistently and effectively. Of course, all the client's expectations are important, but the foundation of the HPI leader's success is his or her ability to partner; deliver low-cost, high-quality products; and be responsive to client needs. Practitioners need to see that the HPI leader has a vision for the future. They are concerned that the HPI leader will look out for their welfare by caring for them as individuals and by investing in their development. Clients and practitioners want to see leadership and commitment that is aligned with the new vision of the HPI department.

Competencies and Experience Necessary for the HPI Leader

How do client and practitioner expectations of the HPI leader affect the identification of competencies and experience required for the position? Table 2-2 lists some of the leadership experience and competencies that may be considered by organizations selecting an HPI leader. A more detailed understanding of how these competencies are applied by an HPI leader may assist the organization in preparing and implementing a more successful selection process.

Table 2-1. Expectations of the HPI leader.

Client Expectations	HPI Practitioner Expectations
• Be committed to the success of the client. • Be proactive as a business partner. • Anticipate and work through resistance to change. • Deliver low-cost, high-quality products. • Be adaptable; do what it takes to win. • Be responsive with timely solutions of the highest quality. • Focus on solutions to problems.	• Be committed to caring for and developing your team members. • Have a vision and a plan. • Anticipate and work through barriers to the team's success. • Obtain the resources needed to do the job. • Listen to new ideas and involve the team. • Respond to the performance needs and requests for help by team members. • Focus solutions and resources on root causes to problems.

Table 2-2. Critical leadership experience and competencies for HPI leaders.

HPI Leader Experiences	HPI Leader Competencies
• line manager of a business unit or sales and service management function • management of a major HPI function • proven ability to successfully navigate complex business/political issues • consistent achievement of multiyear business goals, sales, and/or service results • evidence of passion and commitment for HPI • successful leadership of organizational change as measured by quantitative criteria • prior leadership of strong, highly motivated teams • effective management of profit plans • demonstration of absolute integrity • history of good partnerships with managers and practitioners • formal education	• strategic thinking and vision • skilled in communications, oral and written • knowledge of measurement (evaluation) • project management skills • change management proficiency • process and/or HPI intervention expertise • partnering and relationship-building finesse • leadership expertise • minimum of application-level proficiency in performance consulting competencies

STRATEGIC THINKING AND VISION. The HPI department operates at its highest potential when its goals, products, and services are aligned with the organization's business strategy and HPI process. This alignment occurs when the HPI leader and senior managers share a common vision and strategy for performance improvement. The opportunity lies in helping the HPI function managers and senior line managers create this vision and translate it into support for the new process and HPI department. A great deal of the HPI leader's success depends on making the HPI process and structure fit the organization's business model, strategic direction, and culture.

The HPI leader creates and communicates the HPI vision as a road map for implementing the change to one process and one HPI function. The vision articulates what is different in creating a new performance improvement process, organization, and change in HPI practitioner expectations. It defines for clients and HPI practitioners the value added by the new process and department. The vision involves a radical change for the HPI functions, which will no longer operate in silos or compete for ownership of the client. It serves as a benchmark by which HPI practitioners can measure results and gauge quality of services. The vision has as its foundation a process model that translates the words in the vision statement into practical actions supporting the business.

SKILLED IN COMMUNICATION. The HPI leader seizes every opportunity to communicate what the team is going to do and how the team is going to do it. The leader frequently talks and writes about why change is necessary, how it is progressing, and where the team is going. This approach by the HPI leader helps practitioners warm up to the changes in progress. The issue here isn't about being a master communicator—it's about the willingness to be open, honest, and caring enough to share thoughts and listen to the thoughts of others. There can be no surprises.

KNOWLEDGE OF MEASUREMENT. The HPI leader is responsible for adding value to the clients, the organization, and the HPI department. This requires a leader with sophistication in measurement (evaluation) of comprehensive performance interventions. The HPI leader must be conversant with a variety of metrics that enjoy credibility with clients and HPI practitioners. Just as business units are held accountable for success, the HPI leader must hold the HPI department to the same standard. (See chapter 10 for the HPI scorecard.)

PROJECT MANAGEMENT SKILLS. The HPI leader demonstrates expertise in building teams for planning, implementing, and measuring projects. These may involve single business units or they may yield organization-wide results. Effective project management is a competency that is often lacking in organizations but one that is a critical element for the HPI leader to achieve early credibility and success in the organization.

CHANGE MANAGEMENT PROFICIENCY. The change to one HPI process is a marathon of 3 to 5 years; it is not a sprint. The HPI leader must be sensitive to the level of effort required by practitioners to make this change a reality while satisfying the aggressive demands of supporting the business. Practitioners are going to need time to work through their fear of change. They need to see that the HPI leader's approach to change won't add significantly to existing workloads. Going slowly early in the transition builds the working relationships needed for later accelerated breakthroughs in performance.

PROCESS AND/OR HPI INTERVENTION EXPERTISE. The HPI leader with experience and competencies in any of the HPI functions—OD, TQM, process reengineering, IT, or instructional systems design—brings technical credibility to the position. Understanding the role and contributions of each HPI function in working together to bring complete solutions to client performance problems is essential. The HPI leader needs working expertise with a performance improvement process model. This involves experience in using that model in a complete intervention with clients.

PARTNERING AND RELATIONSHIP-BUILDING FINESSE. The HPI leader's foundation for the successful change to performance consulting lies in the partnerships created and maintained with key stakeholders. Key stakeholders are line managers who become HPI clients with the credibility, influence, resources, and decision-making authority to be early champions of the new process.

They are the ones with business needs and are willing to take the risk in sponsoring a HPI project. These relationships with key clients are created and sustained based on mutual trust and respect. The vision, business rationale, and approach to creating this new way of doing business must be so compelling and clear that it sells itself.

The HPI leader must influence clients to buy performance consulting based on its benefits using the same approach to selling any other business product or service. The leader has to identify the audience, identify key clients, determine their needs, and communicate the benefits of HPI products and services. The HPI leader will succeed who "underpromises" and "overdelivers" with a quality and timeliness that delights the client. The intervention needs to be planned for a quick turnaround. Communication skills are vital to debrief the client frequently and share best practices within the consulting team as they occur. These small successes create a ripple effect that builds credibility and a demand for more consulting services.

Key stakeholders also include the HPI practitioners. The HPI leader treats each HPI practitioner as a key client for purposes of changing to a new process. Each HPI practitioner is treated with respect, as a professional, with the integrity and intelligence to be an equal partner in creating a new future. Practitioners are assigned responsibility for creating the vision and in serving as change agents. The HPI leader should focus practitioners on using the new HPI process for achieving early successes.

When it comes to change, the faint of heart will surface. The successful HPI leader expects and plans for strong resistance that may spring up when integrating practitioners into a new department. The HPI leader will encounter the passion and ownership of HPI practitioners within their silos and single-focus process models. The successful HPI leader is resilient in the face of adversity and persistent in doing what is right for the organization, the client, and the HPI team. Negotiation is a skill that the HPI leader must fine-tune to break down resistance. (See chapter 7 on partnering and contracting.)

LEADERSHIP EXPERTISE. By setting an example as a change leader, the HPI leader demonstrates the passion and courage to lead the change to performance improvement. He or she models the new performance expectations, values, and behaviors expected of each practitioner. The HPI leader is among the first to tackle learning and applying the new performance consulting process. This includes making mistakes and expecting others to make mistakes in learning new competencies. The HPI leader lives the vision, and talks and acts in accordance with its values.

Leaders can build HPI practitioner commitment by modeling their own commitment to the HPI process and structure by actively embracing the change. Over time the combination of early successes and client support increases the likelihood of creating a unified HPI department. This happens when clients and HPI practitioners believe that the whole is greater than the sum of its parts. The HPI leader enrolls and commits practitioners to the process through their creative involvement in building each phase of the process. He or she serves as a guide, coach, and a mentor.

Successful HPI leaders know and use available resources. They can tap into the pool of practitioners in the organization and the marketplace to find those who possess needed competencies and experience. They are able to find projects where there is a business rationale for mutual support. Additional strategies include partnering one of the HPI practitioners with an external partner and being clear up front about how all stakeholders can win.

An essential role of the HPI leader is to recognize the dedication and results of practitioners as they change their professional way of life. It is not an easy road to follow. The HPI leader should celebrate small wins and new skills, and provide recognition—publicly, privately, loudly, and with fanfare.

Behavioral Selection

It is essential that interviewing and testing for behaviors be a strong component of the leader-selection process. This involves determining the behaviors that enhance the leader's potential for success as well as those behaviors that are considered barriers. If any of these behaviors as barriers are detected, it doesn't automatically mean that the candidate should not be hired (figure 2-1). Rather, it is important to understand these behavioral gaps for the position and determine whether there is willingness among senior management to help the incumbent. If this is the case, then the individual is selected based on the mutual understanding of the behaviors in question and a commitment made for an initial development plan.

Action Step 3: Identify Practitioners Willing to Serve

The role of the practitioner as influence leader is essential to the successful change to performance consulting. There are too many products and services to be designed, developed, and delivered, and too much to be learned, and too many clients to work with, for one HPI leader to successfully make the integration of HPI functions a reality. What can practitioners do in this role to support the change to one HPI process? It has everything to do with establishing credibility for the new HPI department through new behaviors and approaches with peers and clients. Practitioners accomplish this by

> ✦ serving as agents of change in partnering and communicating with clients, with an emphasis on identifying manageable client needs and linking the features and benefits of HPI department products and services to these client business needs for early wins

Figure 2-1. HPI leader behaviors to avoid.

GLORY HOUND: Takes all of the credit and is constantly self-promoting.	**HYPERACTIVE:** Lacks the calm, reassuring demeanor of a senior manager by acting as if every issue is a crisis.	**INCONSISTENT:** Is unfocused, constantly thinking up and acting on new ideas before implementing those already in progress.
IMPERSONAL: Is unable to relate to people on a human level; every interaction must have a business purpose.	**LACKS HUMILITY:** Is egocentric, knows all the answers and never fails to remind you of that fact.	**QUESTIONABLE VALUES:** Plays politics at the expense of doing what is right and gives different answers to the same question depending on who is asking.

+ identifying opportunities for achieving small but meaningful changes in the business unit work environment that will help employees work through barriers to performance
+ being service quality role models in providing clients with the highest quality of responsive and proactive support.
+ conducting the business of HPI with the highest professionalism, demonstrating superior business practices and behaviors
+ getting in the habit of measuring and communicating HPI successes using concepts and terms that clients understand and find credible.

Not every practitioner will feel comfortable serving as a change agent. The role requires the willingness to take risks based on the belief that implementing the vision, HPI products and services, and the new, unified HPI process is the right thing to do for employees, clients, and the organization. Working with the HPI leader and managers of the functions, the practitioner as change agent becomes a force multiplier in spreading the good news and serving as an advocate for HPI.

Action Step 4: Create an Organizational and Cultural Integration Plan

Finding an individual with these competencies and behaviors to be the HPI leader is a tall order. Once this individual is selected, it is essential that a plan of action be developed for the first 90 days to maximize opportunities for future success. An important part of this plan is to factor in CEO and executive support to help the new HPI leader avoid potential land mines and quickly assimilate into the culture of the organization. This is important because the HPI leader is coming into the organization in a change-agent role that may not always be welcome.

Table 2-3 lists some of the tasks and outcomes that the HPI leader needs to include in an initial 90-day plan. The specifics of such a plan need to be customized to the vision, culture, strategic direction, and goals of the organization and the sense of urgency established by the CEO. This plan should be developed through a series of meetings called by the HPI leader and attended by key stakeholders, members of senior management, HPI managers, and key clients. The development of this plan becomes a joint venture in successfully launching the new HPI leader and the change process within HPI.

Action Step 5: Identify Performance Expectations and Early Measures of Success

The selection team establishes an initial set of high-level performance outcomes that are reviewed and approved by the CEO and other key stakeholders. The purpose of developing these tentative outcomes is to focus the efforts of the selection team on business imperatives that need to be factored into the selection profile. The HPI leader modifies these outcomes with the CEO and key stakeholders as part of his or her 90-day plan.

The performance outcomes for the first year may involve internal HPI changes in building process, organizational structure, and performer readiness. There may be outcomes relating to improving client satisfaction, establishing partnerships, and conducting limited performance interventions. The HPI leader often uses this list of outcomes to begin crafting a personal balanced scorecard that later becomes part of the HPI organization's scorecard as outlined in chapter 10 of this book.

This personal balanced scorecard should also contain behavioral outcomes. Because the HPI leader's success largely depends on the behaviors demonstrated in leading organizational change, the effectiveness of the HPI leader goes beyond competencies and experience. Selecting the right HPI leader is also a quest to see if the applicant's behaviors fit the culture and values—the norms—expected of leaders in the organization. It requires careful consideration of the alignment between the behaviors and actions of the applicant and the potential willingness of practitioners to be led by this individual. The HPI leader's behavioral outcomes need to be positively stated to fit the cultural expectations of the organization as suggested in table 2-3.

Table 2-3. HPI leader's 90-day plan: tasks and outcomes.

Task	Outcomes
Attend orientation	Complete administrative in-processing, learn the history and organizational structure, and learn employee issues and concerns
Review organization's vision, values, strategic plans, goals, and current organizational performance	Be able to explain the leadership vision and organizational values, strategies and goals by line of business, and results achieved to date
CEO introduces HPI leader to executive management	Establish HPI leader role clarity, expectations and need for senior management support
Develop a CEO support plan	Identify the actions, resources, and CEO support necessary for the HPI leader to successfully transition into the organization
Schedule meetings with the CEO, key clients, executive team, HPI managers and practitioners, service partners, and suppliers	Establish rapport, discuss current status and needs, present a new vision for HPI functions, and identify partnership opportunities
Schedule periodic follow-up meetings with CEO and senior management	Improve communication, coordination of plans and initiatives, and strengthen relationships
Set initial goals with direct reports and progress review meetings	Establish initial performance management practices and standards within the HPI department
Conduct a high level assessment of HPI capabilities	Determine practitioner capabilities, scope and effectiveness of processes, models and tools, organizational effectiveness of structure, and client satisfaction with HPI products and services
Create a plan for developing the HPI transition plan	Gain approval by key stakeholders on the steps necessary to create an integrated HPI approach

Action Step 6: Decide Whether to Seek Candidates Internally or Externally

Should the HPI leader be hired from within or is it a better strategy to go outside and bring in fresh blood? There are passionate advocates for each approach. Certainly internal hires are a known quantity, but they may lack some of the critical experience and skills expected of an HPI leader. Though it is not uncommon for internal hires to demonstrate new behaviors and actions when they receive the mantle of authority, external hires are a bigger issue because their past behaviors and actions are harder to identify. Whether the leader is selected from within or without, if behaviors are not carefully weighed in the selection decision, then there is higher potential for failure.

Table 2-4 provides a list of advantages and disadvantages to internal versus external hires. Certainly, potential HPI leaders can be found in the marketplace, but they are expensive and hard to find. The HPI leader is a hybrid—an individual with line experience, instincts, and a history of results behind his or her credibility as an HPI practitioner.

If the selection team and hiring manager decide to hire externally, then it may be advisable to engage a search firm. Search firms need to be hired with much the same care as an executive for the organization. Referrals and references are needed. The culture, methodology, and style of the search firm must be aligned with the hiring organization. The search firm must be clear that this is not a typical hiring engagement. The firm must completely understand the nontraditional background, competencies, and experiences of the HPI leader that are required for success. The search consultants must be closely partnered with the selection team for the search to be fruitful.

The search consultants need to spend time with and interview HPI practitioners and clients in the organization to truly understand the HPI functions the incumbent will be leading. Interviews with senior managers will help the search consultants understand client performance expectations and the amount of change involved in the HPI leader's job. The search consultants need access to several critical documents:

✦ selection profile
✦ key performance goals for the first 6 months

Table 2-4. Selecting the HPI leader: internal or external hire?

	Advantages	Disadvantages
Internal Hire	• understands the organization's culture, values, and approaches to the business • knows the players within the organization and the HPI functions • little lag time required in moving the change process forward.	• past successes and sins known to everyone within the organization and may carry old baggage into a new job • may experience resistance and resentment from former peers • may lack the formal commitment and mandate for change from senior management due to a "business as usual" mentality associated with a known player • may be selected because a home needs to be found for this person or because of salary constraints or to save on relocation costs.
External Hire	• brings new ideas, approaches, and experiences to the organization • honeymoon with senior management provides a jump-start of resources and support for the change process • doesn't have a negative bias on what is possible	• lag time in learning the culture, values, and "land mines" in the organization • needs to learn the players and establish effective networks. • must establish credibility with senior management, peers, and the HPI practitioners through early wins.

✦ current HPI functions organizational chart and information on products and services

✦ the selection team's expectations on candidate background reviews, interviews, timelines, and communication updates.

Another consideration is that individuals fitting the selection profile tend to be hard to find and expensive. Their personality and leadership profiles often indicate that they will make change happen but will also move on after 2 or 3 years to the next challenge in a new organization. Considering these circumstances, many selection teams are taking the approach of growing their own HPI leaders from within the organization. They tend to compromise on the selection criteria and hire from within one who is the closest fit in terms of the experience, competencies, and behaviors needed for the position.

Progress Milestones

If you are willing to provide leadership for organizational change, then you must be willing to stake your personal credibility in leading the integration of the HPI department into a new process, new organizational structure, new roles, and competencies. Your statements and actions must be aligned if HPI practitioners from diverse functions are to be expected to take the first risky and anxiety-producing steps in changing skills and behaviors. Taking risks is the responsibility of formal leaders, such as the HPI leader and function managers, and practitioners serving as influence leaders. This is the price of success.

The role of the HPI leader is that of an integrator of process, as a visionary thinker and communicator. The HPI leader must have the capacity for translating the HPI process into an implementation plan and actions. Being the champion of the development and learning of competencies requires the HPI leader and function managers to be the first to recognize that their skills must change, and then they must take steps to do something about it. The HPI leader's role as a change manager dictates a role with equal parts of strategic partner, tactical executor, and team player to integrate the new, unified HPI process effectively. The HPI leader persistently works with all stakeholders on the need to change the work environment as a basis for sustainable performance improvement.

In the next chapter, you will learn how to actually begin building your new HPI department.

Key Points of This Chapter

✓ Include all key stakeholders as members of the selection team with a highly respected member of senior management serving as the team leader.

✔ Build an HPI leader selection profile to carefully identify the competencies and behaviors required for success and then use it as the primary criterion for the selection decision.

✔ Be clear about the performance expectations for the position held by the CEO and other key stakeholders and factor those criteria into the selection profile.

✔ Give individual practitioners the opportunity to become actively involved in the selection process, communicate frequently on progress, and reinforce their role as influence leaders for change within HPI.

✔ Create an action plan for the HPI leader's first 90 days that is supported by the CEO and key members of executive management.

Organizing for Success

Getting your organization to make any type of radical change is not easy and oftentimes may seem impossible. Asking your organization to get out of comfortable silos and deal with performance issues may be even more of a challenge. This part of the book will give you the tools necessary to get a new cross-functional, HPI-focused program up and running. Take a look at the goals for part two of this book:

1. Use a process of partnering, assessment, and action planning to build a new HPI department.
2. Create a department structure with executive and HPI practitioner support that serves as an enhancer to improved performance.
3. Build an internal HPI network and establish external alliances for collaboration on joint HPI projects and the sharing of resources to maximize the impact of the HPI department in your organization.
4. Build an integrated HPI process through the efforts of practitioners from all of the HPI functions. Use cross-functional teams to identify best practices and menus of tools that will provide complete performance solutions for clients.
5. Develop a strategy for the transition of practitioner roles and competencies through formal and workplace learning opportunities.
6. The HPI leader and function managers create a work environment supportive of practitioner workshop attendance and on-the-job development of performance improvement competencies.

31

These goals represent important decisions that must be made during the transition process. Goals 1 and 2 are covered in chapter 3 ("Building the New HPI Department"), goal 3 is addressed in chapter 4 ("Creating Networks and Alliances"), goal 4 is the topic of chapter 5 ("Rallying the Organization, Building the Process"), and goals 5 and 6 are addressed in chapter 6 ("Changing Practitioner Skills and Knowledge"). After you have your "arms" around the scope of the work, read the chapters in this part for details on how to actually accomplish your goals. At the end of each chapter in this section, you will find another checklist to help you monitor your progress and transition to the next step in the process.

Building the New HPI Department

How you as the HPI leader or as a practitioner approach the task of integrating functions, processes, and practitioners for a mutually supporting HPI department makes all the difference. Clients and practitioners tend to be skeptical of proclamations announcing the change to a new department with no new products and services to offer. They want to see results directly linked to the change in HPI focus before accepting claims of benefits to be realized by the new HPI department. The five action steps for this chapter provide you with points to consider when building an HPI department that fits the business and performance needs of your organization.

Action Steps for Creating a Unified HPI Function

1. Conduct an environmental scan of the organization to plan and build a new HPI department by identifying and partnering with key clients, assessing needs and capabilities, and implementing actions.
2. Decide which type of department structure—centralized or decentralized—that you will create.
3. Get a senior executive sponsor, preferably the CEO.
4. Build an advisory group from among the key stakeholders in the organization.
5. Create a department infrastructure with the flexibility to provide client performance support appropriate for complete solutions to improve performance.

Action Step 1: Conduct an Environmental Scan of the Organization

The HPI leader needs a systematic approach to creating the new HPI department that may satisfy clients and practitioners. Table 3-1 contains a broad overview of a three-phase model that can be used in building a new

HPI process and department. It provides clients, practitioners, and the HPI leader with a general approach to working together in overcoming the barriers of silos and self-interest to merge processes and functions. You will find more help in chapters 4, 5, and 6, which provide a detailed examination of how to build the new HPI process, the department structure, and prepare performers to be performance consultants. For now, concentrate on understanding the big organizational picture. Table 3-1 outlines a three-phase approach to help you organize your thinking and move to the next steps outlined in the book. More detail on the three phases follow this table.

Phase I: Identify and Partner with Key Clients

The HPI leader must partner with functional managers and key clients on a common vision, goals, and then communication of a plan for the integration of all HPI functions. The managers and practitioners in OD and quality are natural allies for the HPI leader in working through the integration process. You should move forward with this partnership before formally raising the question on integration. Even more important is enlisting the support of one or several highly credible executives for the creation of the unified HPI department and asking them to serve as advocates for building and using a new HPI process.

As the HPI leader, it is your job to schedule detailed planning meetings with key stakeholders. The goal of your initial meeting is to get all participants to agree in principle that forming one department and one HPI process is in the best interests of clients, the organization, and all the HPI functions. Make sure you invite the CEO or a senior executive to attend this initial planning meeting to talk about the business necessity of moving out of silos and creating a new HPI department. Nothing works better than the presence of a CEO or senior executive to bring reluctant parties to the table.

The outcomes of the partnering phase are to establish working relationships among the key stakeholders and create a contract that outlines an approach to build one HPI department. Follow-up meetings from this initial meeting should have the following outcomes:

+ creation of a vision statement that unifies all of the HPI functions around a common purpose
+ a systematic investigation of how the HPI functions might work together to integrate models, tools, terminology and resources
+ an assessment of the gaps in the HPI functions' process models, tools, and capabilities to support the vision and client needs
+ development of specific actions to build the new HPI department and close the department's capability gaps

Table 3-1. A three-phase approach for creating the new HPI department.

Phase I Identify and Partner	Phase II Assessment	Phase III Implement Actions
Create the HPI department's: • Vision • Initial goals • Communication plan • Planning meetings • Contract for next steps	Identify gaps and causes: • Function HPI capabilities • Practitioner skills/knowledge • Function process models • Function tools and terms • Contract with functions on transition plan	Plan, develop, and implement: Client actions • Identify line champions • Identify performance gaps • Contract for early wins Plan, develop, and implement: HR actions • Competency model • Selection profiles • Job descriptions • Reward/recognition model Plan, develop, and implement: Learning actions • Workshops • Consulting team roles • Coaching Plan, develop, and implement: Work environment actions • HPI process • Department structure • Policies/procedures • HPI performance scorecard

◆ building and implementation of a transition plan, timelines, and accountabilities within the organization

◆ development of a communication strategy about the new department and its capabilities.

All these goals are critical to the success of building and launching the new department. One goal—creating the department's overall vision—is the foundation on which all the other goals depend. You should anticipate devoting several of your early meetings to creating an HPI vision statement. Developing a vision statement is hard, conceptual work that some practitioners find difficult. As the HPI leader, you may consider writing a draft statement and distribute it for review before the meeting. Giving each HPI practitioner time to think about how this statement represents the purpose and added value of the new department will help jump-start this meeting. Here's a sample draft vision statement:

> *The future of the HPI department is in serving as the champion of the employee and as a results-oriented partner with management sharing a common goal of organizational success. We operate at a strategic level in discussing client business goals, issues, and strategies. We also operate at a tactical level when analyzing specific performance problems and implementing interventions. We organize teams of consultants and specialists who can identify the root causes of performance problems and describe the desired state if performance is to improve. We implement appropriate solutions with a service quality that delights the client. The key to our success is in partnering with clients around a common performance improvement process that we embrace as one team.*

Hammering out a vision statement that is acceptable to all of the HPI functions is a process of negotiation and consensus. You might want to consider the use of a neutral facilitator or external partner to help give the process the objectivity needed to move forward. Once you have finalized this statement with the input of the CEO and senior line champion(s), this statement will be the anchor of the new department. It defines what is different about the HPI department and becomes the glue to bind practitioners together and break down existing silos.

Phase II: Assessment

The contract developed during the partnering phase lists the responsibilities and approaches to assessment needed for building one process and a new HPI department. A cross-functional team is formed of practitioners from all the HPI functions to collect data on the process models, tools, function organizational structures, performance expectations and competencies from internal HPI functions and in the marketplace. This assessment of each HPI function's capabilities and practitioner skills is needed to identify common ground for building the new department. Team members gather data through a review of documentation and reports. External data on best practices in HPI are collected from professional associations, external partners, and a review of the literature. Interviews, surveys, and focus groups are conducted often with exemplary practitioners from each HPI function to identify best practices in models, concepts, tools, and terminology. Practitioners complete a survey on their strengths, developmental opportunities, consulting related skills, and experience. Questions are also asked about the current performance of each HPI function and opinions requested on how each HPI function adds value in creating a new HPI process.

The data is sorted, analyzed, and summarized with objectivity by the HPI cross-functional team. A data-reporting meeting to review and discuss the team's summary report is attended by the HPI leader, function managers, and key clients. The key client(s) provides a business reality check on the data. The data is reported and discussed with objectivity. The outcome of this meeting is a contract among the HPI managers and practitioners to develop a series of actions and a plan for creating the HPI department.

Phase III: Implement Actions

The consulting intervention to build the new HPI department involves a number of mutually supporting actions with a cross-functional team assigned to develop each action. The cross-functional teams allow practitioners to break out of their silos and work together in building the new department process, structure, products, and services. A master plan for the intervention is developed around four key actions:

CLIENT ACTIONS. The HPI leader discusses with potential clients the vision, mission, and value added by the new HPI department. He or she markets the change to HPI with strong emphasis on the benefits and results for clients and practitioners. Clients willing to partner with the HPI leader are identified for quick turnaround interventions that can become early wins for the client, the new HPI process, and the unified department.

HUMAN RESOURCES ACTIONS. A competency model becomes the practitioner's blueprint on the new jobs and roles in the HPI department. The skills, knowledge, experience, and behaviors are clearly specified in the competency model for each new job and role. The model is also used to build selection profiles, job descriptions, and new compensation plans for practitioner reward and recognition. The competency model helps department managers and team leaders identify the need for new skills in matrix management and in using tools for the motivation, reward, recognition, and development of their practitioners. An orientation for new department members is developed on the new vision, mission, department units and teams, competencies, and departmental operating policies and procedures.

LEARNING ACTIONS. Often the HPI leader is in the position of internally growing the talent for the new department because it is very difficult to find ready-made performance consultants in the marketplace. This becomes an excellent opportunity to begin the integration of HPI practitioners around a common set of competencies and developmental experiences. For many practitioners this is the first time the organization has actually invested time and money in their development. Practitioners are expected to attend workshops and then are assigned to a consulting team to apply their new skills and knowledge with the support of an experienced coach.

There are several questions that the HPI leader needs to think through while wisely investing scarce resources for the competency development of practitioners.

- ✦ Which new skills and knowledge are needed by the HPI leader and managers to lead the practitioners to achieve new levels of desired performance?
- ✦ Which practitioner skills and knowledge are required to support the client's business needs?
- ✦ What feedback are practitioners provided to support the desired performance?
- ✦ What motivates team members to take ownership of achieving the desired performance?
- ✦ How do practitioners take advantage of learning opportunities provided by the department while taking initiative for their development?

WORK ENVIRONMENT ACTIONS. The implementation of actions to build a unified HPI process and department requires a change in the practitioner's work environment to break down existing silos. Cross-functional teams are formed to create a new HPI process and a flexible department structure designed to support the new process, roles, and performance expectations required to integrate HPI functions effectively. An essential component of the HPI process is a comprehensive measurement model designed as a balanced performance scorecard.

Action Step 2: Make a Decision—Centralized or Decentralized Department

The way the department is organized can be either an enhancer or a barrier to unifying the HPI functions and implementing performance consulting. A properly designed structure evolves and keeps abreast of the rapidly changing business and performance needs of the organization. What this structure looks like varies. The uniqueness of the culture of one organization may lead to the success of a structure that would fail in another organization.

Should a centralized or decentralized approach be used to organize the department? Each approach has its proponents who present convincing arguments on the benefits of one over the other. Leaders in HPI have successfully integrated functions using either a centralized or decentralized department. In some organizations, variations of both approaches are blended into a hybrid model. Beginning with a centralized HPI department often works best to enhance the early integration and implementation of the new HPI process. The reality is that in its evolution most departments move back and forth between centralized and decentralized structures. Human performance improvement leaders and practitioners need to be comfortable and effective in supporting client's needs regardless of the organizational approach currently in use by the HPI functions.

In a centralized department, all HPI resources, personnel, budget, equipment, and facilities are the direct responsibility of the HPI leader. A centralized structure provides maximum flexibility for the HPI leader regarding the availability and use of resources. Common goals and priorities are set. The HPI leader integrates and assigns resources. Efficiencies are realized by eliminating duplication of services. Effectiveness of HPI products and services delivered to clients is often improved by eliminating competition for client ownership and integrating HPI competencies into a more comprehensive menu of tools.

The HPI leaders in a centralized HPI department can adjust the structure of the department based on resource assumptions and their assessment of the type of structure needed to achieve the performance expectations of the organization. In a smaller department, for example, the HPI leader may combine the performance services and consulting services teams. Regardless of the size of the department, the administrative and consulting teams need to be separate because of their distinct competencies and roles. Nevertheless, they must be coordinated as mutually supporting arms of the HPI department.

In the decentralized approach, core functions that are needed to support enterprisewide performance report to the HPI leader. A business-unit-specific team is assigned to each line of business to support the client's unique business and performance needs. Although early success can be achieved by using a decentralized departmental structure, integrating HPI functions and processes is a long endeavor, often requiring a more bureaucratic approach. Human performance improvement functions report to various business and staff units with different priorities, goals, resources, and capabilities. This structure facilitates active involvement of line managers through their ownership of HPI assets. Line managers usually take a more active role in understanding capabilities, providing resources, and using HPI practitioners to solve performance problems.

Line ownership, however, may have a disadvantage. Clients often focus on single-event, short-term fixes rather than on longer-term solutions. The HPI leaders often experience difficulty in getting priority for access to personnel and resources needed for organization-wide HPI interventions.

Action Step 3: Get a Senior Executive Sponsor

Organizations need specialists who are experts in specific areas and who know more about a topic than anyone else in the organization does. Line managers want to use the expertise of these specialists to resolve difficult problems. Human performance problems are dynamic and complex. Therefore, the efforts of the specialists must be coordinated through an individual who truly understands the big picture, including the business, processes, and performers. This individual must be appropriately placed within the organization to have the influence and credibility necessary for success (LaBonte & Robinson, 1999).

The ideal reporting arrangement for the HPI leader is to the CEO or president of the organization. The CEO provides the support needed for the strategic alignment of the HPI process with the organization's business model, purpose and values. The CEO can provide the breathing room needed in a start-up situation by communicating reasonable expectations for the new department. This creates the time and opportunity needed to build the process, structure, and performer skills for achieving early wins.

The HPI leader and the CEO need to invest time in each other. Building the relationship, understanding the priorities and business needs of the CEO, and establishing a working routine that works for both are some of the HPI leader's early objectives. The HPI leader needs to educate the CEO on how the new process and department add value to the organization. This level of understanding is critical for the CEO to serve as the chair of the HPI advisory group and to take a leadership role in developing the purpose and agenda and selecting members for the first advisory group meeting.

Action Step 4: Build an Advisory Group

The purpose of the advisory group is to assist the HPI leader in developing the vision, strategic alignment, and priorities for the new HPI department. The advisory group comprises senior managers who take an organization-wide view of the HPI department, its capabilities, and its role as a strategic performance improvement resource. Its leadership is crucial in breaking down the HPI function's silos and eliminating potential turf wars.

The CEO or president often serves as the advisory group chair. The chair extends a personal invitation to the heads of the major business units to participate. In some cases, these business unit leaders may previously have had one of the HPI functions directly reporting to them. Participation in the advisory group helps the business unit managers get over any feeling of loss. It allows them to continue their ownership of performance improvement by having a stake in the future of the new HPI department.

The CEO reviews the role of the advisory group at their first meeting. The chair indicates that the group's charter is to serve as guides, mentors, and champions for the new process and department. An important win at this first meeting is consensus on the advisory group charter. The advisory group charter often involves identifying resources for the HPI department and reviewing how resources are prioritized against business needs. The group is a valuable source of input on the development of the HPI scorecard and its alignment with organizational measures of success. The advisory group also becomes an important sounding board to resolve conflicts. It becomes a forum to discuss issues and avoid one-on-one clashes with clients that could seriously damage relationships.

The advisory group charter further states that they provide strategic direction, focus, and priorities in support of organizational and business unit goals. This involves ensuring that the HPI department:

- ✦ supports the vision and values of the organization in all products and services
- ✦ coordinates and reconciles organization-wide goals with business unit goals and HPI department priorities
- ✦ reviews the value added by the HPI department to the organization
- ✦ takes joint ownership with the HPI leader on the products, services, and results achieved by the HPI department.

The HPI leader may recommend to the advisory board chair that, at a minimum, the board meet semiannually. This recommendation is based on the availability of the senior management team balanced by the HPI leader's need for frequency of support. A breakfast or lunch meeting is usually sufficient. The HPI leader may request that the advisory group meet during the fourth quarter to review year-to-date successes and plan the goals and priorities for the next year. The other meeting is often planned for the beginning of the second quarter to assess early wins and adjust the HPI plan to meet frequently changing organizational needs.

Action Step 5: Create a Department Infrastructure

Action step 2 has a profound bearing on how action step 5 is carried out. How the new, unified HPI department is organized depends on whether the department's infrastructure will be centralized or decentralized. For that reason, this section is divided into two subsections; one is dedicated to a centralized structure, and the other pertains to a decentralized structure.

Centralized Departmental Structure

One approach to overcoming the barriers posed by functions operating in silos is to cluster the administrative and performance improvement functions into separate areas reporting directly to the HPI leader (figure 3-1). The administrative and performance improvement functions usually operate in silos because their day-to-day functions rarely require them to collaborate except for minimal communication. Cross-functional teams link practitioners from each area to corporatewide performance support initiatives. In this way, clients realize the maximum benefit of the full capabilities of the new HPI department. Figure 3-1 depicts a centralized structure for the functions associated with administrative services.

ADMINISTRATIVE SERVICES TEAM. Transactional, daily tasks must be performed to support the business. Administrative specialists, for example, are in employee record keeping, data collection, salary administration, and personnel-related positions. Specialists performing these kinds of administrative tasks are in functions that often measure their success by the timeliness and accuracy of the activity performed. Clustering these administrative services into one team promotes efficiency and effectiveness. It also makes sense based on similarities in competencies, policies, procedures, and technology used for employee support.

Often the backgrounds, capabilities, and professional interests of administrative specialists are such that they do not become performance consultants. The practitioners in administrative functions often see their world in narrowly defined silos. They are often reactive in their approach to the business. The concepts and approaches that are critical to success in HPI are sometimes alien to their perception of value to the organization.

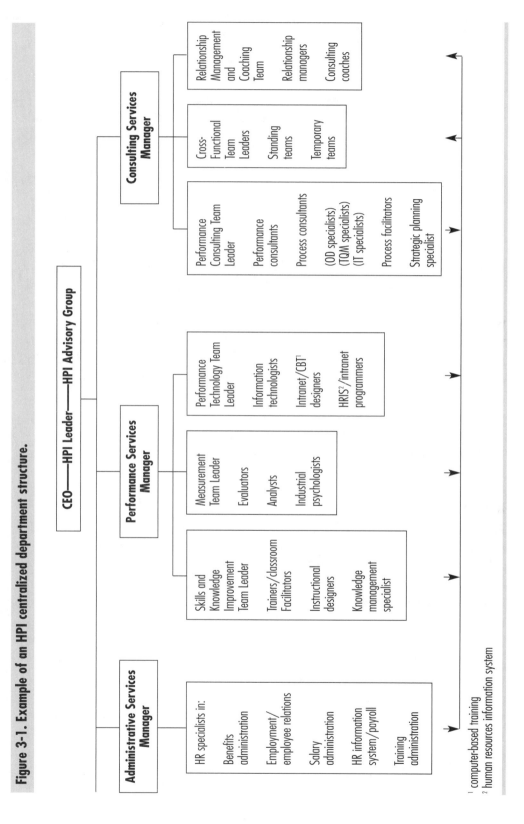

Figure 3-1. Example of an HPI centralized department structure.

CEO——HPI Leader——HPI Advisory Group

Administrative Services Manager

HR specialists in:

Benefits administration

Employment/ employee relations

Salary administration

HR information system/payroll

Training administration

Performance Services Manager

Skills and Knowledge Improvement Team Leader

Trainers/classroom Facilitators

Instructional designers

Knowledge management specialist

Measurement Team Leader

Evaluators

Analysts

Industrial psychologists

Performance Technology Team Leader

Information technologists

Intranet/CBT[1] designers

HRIS[2]/intranet programmers

Consulting Services Manager

Performance Consulting Team Leader

Performance consultants

Process consultants

(OD specialists) (TQM specialists) (IT specialists)

Process facilitators

Strategic planning specialist

Cross-Functional Team Leaders

Standing teams

Temporary teams

Relationship Management and Coaching Team

Relationship managers

Consulting coaches

[1] computer-based training
[2] human resources information system

It is usually not productive for the HPI leader to spend a great deal of time and resources early in the integration working on learning the new HPI process with these specialists. Instead, the leader should work with them in creating the new departmental structure without initially changing a great deal of what they do on a daily basis. This approach works well to gain early buy-in and create time to build the new HPI department and process. The initial focus should be on the performance functions in which practitioners have the experience and perspective to make the HPI process a reality. After the department is functioning with performance consulting wins in place is the time to work on the perspective and skills of the administrative specialists.

Don't make the mistake of writing off the involvement of administrative specialists in the HPI process! The HPI leader ensures that everyone has a role in supporting performance consulting. Administrative specialists often have skills that are valuable in supporting HPI. They tend to be analytical and attentive to detail and work with data. They are also people-oriented and often demonstrate excellent service quality behaviors. With proper preparation, these specialists can work on cross-functional teams as interviewers, data analysts, and project leaders. They often can serve as facilitators of new employee orientation and as relationship managers. The key for the HPI leader is to pick the right time, appropriate roles, and preparation necessary for administrative specialists and practitioners in other teams to participate in the HPI process. This has to be orchestrated so that it does not add significantly to an already heavy workload. Careful scheduling, innovative uses of technology, and outsourcing help to eliminate time wasters and lower-value tasks. Service quality is maintained while administrative specialists contribute to the HPI mission of the department.

PERFORMANCE SERVICES TEAM. The performance services team designs, develops, and delivers skills and knowledge improvement solutions in training, assessment and testing services, and the collection, sorting, and accessibility of data. These products and services have a dual purpose in serving clients and internal practitioners. Evaluators are part of the team and provide scorecard measures for single-solution activities, such as training, as well as for performance consulting interventions. Team members provide valuable competencies and experience in a variety of roles on consulting cross-functional teams and as coaches and relationship managers.

The relationship managers and coaches are important resources for making this new department more valuable to clients. The relationship manager can ease some of the pain for clients concerned about the centralized department and their perceived loss of control. The relationship manager talks and acts like a member of the client's business unit. The relationship manager helps the client understand the value of organization-wide initiatives supported by the HPI department and how these initiatives benefit the client's business. The proactive approach taken by the relationship manager, the focus on client needs, and the speed and quality of response are important in getting client support for the new HPI department (chapter 7).

CONSULTING SERVICES TEAM. The senior consultants of the HPI department form the consulting services team. These practitioners often have experience in OD, TQM, or consulting. These consultants serve as cross-functional team leaders and relationship managers assigned to key clients. They also have the competencies and experience to be coaches and process facilitators for internal development activities. The team possesses information technology competencies to improve performance through systems reengineering and systems usability testing. Strategic planning specialists assist clients in aligning business unit goals with the strategic direction and business model of the organization.

The team leader has the responsibility for everything the team does or fails to do. The team leader is responsible for performance and salary reviews. He or she helps each team member set goals, provides coaching, and offers rewards and recognition based on results achieved. The team leader is skilled at matrix management, and juggling priorities and resources in the assignment of consultants to other roles and teams.

CROSS-FUNCTIONAL TEAMS. It is essential that the HPI leader involve practitioners from all of the HPI functions in working on performance problems. The ability to support client business needs requires the ability to pull together quickly cross-functional teams with the competencies necessary for quality client support. The team becomes a learning laboratory for the HPI practitioners to gain skills and knowledge from each other while learning the new process. Cross-functional teams are indispensable to the integration of the HPI functions into a new department.

The cross-functional teams are composed of performance consultants and specialists from the administrative and performance services teams. There are often two types of cross-functional teams: temporary and standing. Temporary teams are assigned for interventions supporting one business unit or multiple units when quick turnaround solutions are required. An example of the need for a temporary team is the implementation of a new systems application supporting customer sales and service. The application has a 6-month installation window. The HPI department creates a team involved in the design of the application to ensure that it supports the employee's sales and service performance needs. The team also develops training, work-environment changes in policies and procedures to support employees using the new system, and leader coaching skills and behaviors. Standing teams are dedicated to organization-wide interventions of great impact and long duration. Examples of these interventions include employee retention, implementation of sales and service management processes, and integration of cultures through mergers and acquisitions.

Decentralized Departmental Structure

In a decentralized department, the HPI functions are often organized in silos across a number of departments within an organization. These HPI silos tend to be perpetuated and enhanced by a decentralized approach to organizational structure. The culture and business model of the organization may dictate that a decentralized structure for the HPI department is the approach favored by senior management. If this is the case, then how do the HPI leader and practitioners align the functions properly to balance support for organizational priorities that cut across all lines of business with the specific needs of individual business units? Figure 3-2 depicts a generic model for a decentralized HPI department. (See appendix D if you are interested in creating a university model for a decentralized department.)

ENTERPRISE OR CORPORATE HPI DEPARTMENT. Decentralized structures are more prevalent in larger organizations where the ability of centralized departments is stretched to respond to the urgency of client business needs. Advocates of decentralized HPI structures argue that there are core functions that should be supported by an enterprise HPI department. The remaining functions that deal with business-specific performance support belong in the business unit. The enterprise department contains functions that are directly aligned with the organization's strategic direction, vision, values, and goals. They also are generic functions in that they are not unique to any line of business; they affect all areas of the organization (table 3-2).

BUSINESS UNIT HPI FUNCTIONS. The decentralized structure balances the needs of the enterprise department with the needs of line-of-business HPI support by dedicating departments to business units. From the business unit executive's perspective, a business unit HPI department provides for the appropriate setting of priorities and the efficient use of resources. All initiatives are directly related to core business requirements. Other initiatives are referred to the organizational HPI department, outsourced to an external partner, or eliminated as superfluous. Table 3-3 contains the business unit functions found in many organizations. The HPI focus and client impact of each function are listed.

Figure 3-2. Example of an HPI decentralized department structure.

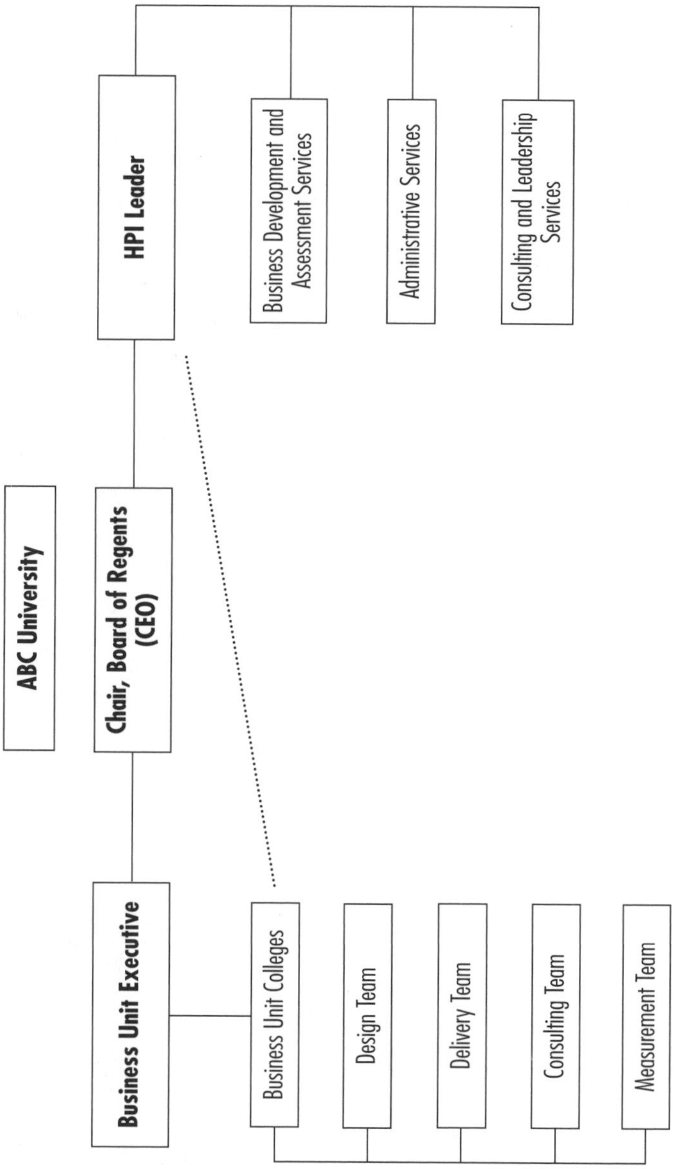

Table 3-2. Enterprise HPI functions (decentralized structure).

Enterprise HPI Department Functions		Client HPI Focus
Administrative Services		Same as discussed for centralized departments (figure 3-1).
Business Development and Assessment Services		The sales arm of the enterprise department, which is responsible for selling and contracting HPI products and services with clients, developing and communicating fees, and supporting shared services agreements.
Consulting and Leadership Services	Succession Planning and Executive Development	Partner with executive management for identifying, assessing, developing, and coaching high potential succession candidates for senior positions.
	Leadership Training and Development	Develop and deliver a core leadership model and competencies that align with the organization's strategies, vision, and values. Provides a pool of skilled leaders capable of creating a positive work environment.
New Employee Orientation		A program that provides general performance expectations and standards for new employees that explains the organizations' culture, structure, sales and service approach, and standards, benefits, and code of conduct. Manager's orientation emphasizes the performance management system, leadership expectations, HR practices, and benefits unique to managers.
Performance Management		This system supports managers and employees setting performance objectives, assessing and planning employee development, coaching, rewarding, and recognizing results. The performance management system is an essential component of the HPI process and must be aligned if sustainable performance improvement is to be achieved.
HPI Process		The HPI process is core to all HPI functions in the organization. The enterprise HPI department coordinates the maintenance and enhancement of the model, conducts workshops to prepare new consultants, and coaches new consultants on using the process.
Performance Consulting		The design, development, and implementation of organization-wide performance consulting interventions are the responsibility of the enterprise HPI department. Interventions may involve changing the work environment to enhance leadership skills and behaviors, establishing and implementing service quality standards, or improving employee retention.
Project Management		The enterprise HPI department provides skilled project managers for organization-wide implementation of special projects. These projects are usually time-sensitive and may involve new systems, models, and approaches that support organizational strategies.

Table 3-3. Business unit HPI functions (decentralized structure).

Business Unit HPI Department Functions		Client HPI Focus
Human Resources Generalists	Employee Selection	Selection models are customized from the performance model and competencies of each position and used to hire the right people for the right job. Effective selection practices are essential for improvements in productivity, efficiency, and quality.
	Incentive Design and Implementation	The organization's performance management system and compensation model provide core templates that are customized to the incentive design requirements of the business unit. Properly designed incentives provide an important source of reward and motivation for employees to improve performance.
Information Technology		This unit provides operational and technical support for business-specific applications, data and management reporting requirements.
Design Team	Instructional Systems Design	Business-unique skills and knowledge training based on competency and performance models are designed in the business unit.
Delivery Team	Employee Training and Development	The delivery of business-specific performance support programs uses a variety of methods that support the needs of clients and performers.
Consulting Team	Performance Consulting	Performance consulting interventions are conducted on performance problems and initiatives that are business-unit specific.
	Project Management	The department provides project managers for the implementation of business-unique products and services.
	Measurement	The team designs measures for client approval as part of the department's HPI scorecard used in determining the success of business unit projects.
	Sales and Service Management	This function comprises the sales, service, and leadership actions that support a business unit's sales and service management process. The sales process must support the organization's sales culture and service quality standards for client referrals and mutual support.

SHARED SERVICES IN DECENTRALIZED ORGANIZATIONS. The decentralized approach is often linked to a shared-services model. In using a shared-services concept, support functions charge the business unit for their products and services. The HPI leader negotiates with the head of each business unit regarding the quantity, quality, timing, and pricing of the core HPI products and services indicated in the contract. This often brings the organizational support functions into competition with each other and with external providers for scarce budget dollars. Line managers pay as they go, demanding quality products and timely delivery.

Traditional support functions, such as HR and training, often are not competitive in a shared-services environment. They often have practitioners who lack the sales and service skills, measurement tools, and products to compete effectively against external providers. External providers not only have a greater array of products and services to offer but usually have economies of scale to undercut internal pricing.

To compete effectively, the HPI department needs to establish an operating model based on the organization's business units. This means that the HPI leader and every practitioner must think and act like business owners. Sales targets, expense goals, and overhead are assigned and must be managed. Practitioners have a stake in the growth and success of the organization. This requires a business model for the HPI department that is built on the following kinds of information:

+ identifying the target audience for HPI products and services
+ identifying potential clients' buying habits and critical business/performance needs
+ identifying external competitors, their competitive advantages and disadvantages
+ building a business model and charging fees appropriately for products and services
+ establishing the HPI department as a profit center and achieving revenue and expense goals
+ establishing procedures and reports needed to track sales, revenue, and expense.

The strongest competitive advantages the HPI department enjoys in a shared-services approach are its client relationships and integrated set of tools supporting the HPI process. The HPI department may undercut the competition in price, but, make no mistake, the HPI department will only stay in business if the quality, timeliness, and impact of its products and services are consistently excellent.

The personal client relationships built over time confer a considerable advantage to the HPI department, imparting knowledge of the business, client needs, and credibility based on prior success. Knowledge of business needs and organizational history gives the HPI leader the edge in customizing actions that add great value to hard-pressed clients searching for results. The integrated capabilities of the HPI process, measurement scorecard, and consulting competencies of the HPI department provide clients with total solutions that many external providers cannot match.

Progress Milestones

In this chapter, you learned about the action steps you must take before your organization can move toward the new HPI model. Here again are the key points to consider from the first four steps in your transition journey discussed in this chapter. In the next chapter, you will learn how to create networks and alliances as opportunities to leverage valuable sources of internal and external expertise and resources that move the transition process forward.

Key Points of This Chapter

- ✔ Be sensitive to change. Take a systematic approach to analyzing your new HPI department's issues and needs.
- ✔ Decide whether your department needs to be centralized or decentralized. You may organize your department around either model or even try a blended approach. However, most HPI departments will eventually operate using the decentralized model.
- ✔ Get strong support from the CEO or president and partner with this leader closely throughout the transition.
- ✔ Make sure you build a highly credible advisory group for your transition process. A strong advisory group is essential to the smooth transition to an integrated HPI function. Remember to involve everyone with a hand in the transition process, from the CEO down to key administrative specialists.
- ✔ Conduct planning meetings with key stakeholders. Get support on HPI department structure, alignment, reporting relationships, and early priorities. Identify business needs and client opportunities for performance consulting.
- ✔ Create a vision statement that all stakeholders have a role in building and agree to.
- ✔ Agree on a plan and HPI model to use in creating the new department.
- ✔ Keep all stakeholders informed.
- ✔ Get as many HPI managers and practitioners as actively involved as possible in creating the new department.

Creating Networks and Alliances

Now that the formal structure of the HPI department has been designed and implemented, you may find that availability of resources becomes an issue. Often HPI departments are constrained by limited resources—lean staffing, meager budgets, facilities, and equipment. There never seems to be enough resources in the profit plan for you to fulfill client demands for support. The costs of designing and developing a new HPI process, tools, and competency models, not to mention preparing practitioners in workshops and on-the-job development, are just a few of your start-up costs for the new department. Clients often have high expectations of performance support that the new HPI department must address if it is to gain and maintain credibility and thrive in a very competitive work environment.

In these situations the HPI leader and practitioners must effectively use the resources directly assigned and also seek and obtain additional support. Getting access to resources external to the department often means that you create partnerships through internal networks and external alliances. Networks and alliances often provide you the additional resources needed in people, budget, equipment, and facilities to support client needs.

Action Steps for Creating New Networks and Alliances

1. Outline the benefits of internal networks and external alliances.
2. Conduct an assessment of resources needed to support organizational and business unit goals and employee performance needs, and identify the resources that are currently available. Evaluate the potential gap.

3. Develop a plan for an internal network and external alliances. Identify and contract with potential partners, roles, and joint ventures. Identify risks, issues, and barriers to success.
4. Measure, communicate, and celebrate joint successes.

This chapter presents an approach for creating an internal HPI network and external alliances for identifying and integrating resources needed to maximize the effectiveness of the new HPI department. This chapter is presented from the perspective of the HPI leader and senior managers and practitioners concerned with planning functions and resource management. The steps listed here provide a starting point for establishing a network and alliances to support your HPI department.

Action Step 1: Outline the Benefits of Internal Networks and External Alliances

The HPI leader is responsible for identifying an approach, a strategy based on leverage points, and partnerships to overcome the potential resource and commitment barriers that are faced by practitioners in the new HPI department. You may encounter resistance from clients and HPI function managers in the business units when it comes to cooperating on joint initiatives or providing resources for enterprisewide projects. A shared-services approach may deny the HPI leader the support of the business unit departments because they likely have different priorities for their resources. When confronted with growing business unit demands, strained resources, and requests from the HPI leader for support, the business unit HPI manager often cannot provide the requested support to the enterprise department. Creating an HPI network of service partners within the organization and alliances with external organizations and agencies is one approach that can overcome the barriers of silos and limited resources.

The HPI leader and practitioners should form teams to brainstorm the benefits of creating an internal network and external alliance for each stakeholder. The stakeholders include your clients, the HPI department and its practitioners, potential internal service partners listed by function, and potential external alliance partners. After this data is sorted and summarized, several individuals representing each stakeholder are contacted to review the data, provide recommendations, and determine the overall validity of conclusions derived from the data. The list of benefits by stakeholder becomes a valuable source of information for developing an effective sales strategy and plan. The HPI leader uses every available means to reinforce the need, value, and benefits of the HPI network including the performance management system, leadership training, orientation, organizational public relations, and media.

Action Step 2: Conduct an Assessment of Resource Needs

What are the resources needed by the HPI department to support critical business needs and expectations, what resources are available, what is the gap, and what can you do about it? These questions form the basis of your resource assessment. Assessing the available resources in people and competencies, products, services and tools, budget, equipment, and facilities becomes the starting point for identifying opportunities to build networks and alliances in support of organizational and business unit goals. Table 4-1 presents one approach to assessing resource needs and opportunities in building networks and alliances. It is based on the assumption that the HPI leader has already started communicating with executive management, HPI practitioners, and with key clients on the concept and benefits.

Action Step 3: Develop a Plan for an Internal Network and External Alliances

Few practitioners have experience in planning and implementing networks within an organization and external alliances. Building a plan of action is

Table 4-1. Assessing resource needs and opportunities.

Assessment Steps	Tasks
Complete a business needs and resources assessment.	• enterprisewide needs and priorities for HPI support • assessment of HPI goals and enterprise needs • HPI available resources
Identify the HPI resources gap.	• staffing and competencies • products, services, and tools • technology, facilities, and equipment budget
Develop a resources plan to close the gap.	• actions needed to obtain resources appropriate to support critical client needs and close gap
Define the HPI network and external alliances.	• vision and purpose • criteria for participation • issues and risks • operating policies and procedures
Conduct an environmental resources scan.	For internal departments and the marketplace: • common areas of mutual interest and needs • benefits of collaborative relationships for all partners • negotiations with senior managers to get HPI assets dedicated to their business units freed up to support enterprisewide HPI initiatives

an essential step to capturing the collective wisdom of the HPI department and potential partners as they share resources and develop successful joint ventures.

The HPI Partner Network

The HPI network is a confederation of internal partners dedicated to supporting each other in improving performance. Internal partners are those functions and practitioners within an organization that have the responsibility to provide products and services to internal clients. These functions can include all of the staff areas in an organization. Some HPI leaders and practitioners fail to consider the support that can be provided by internal partners to the HPI department's mission and goals. Other HPI leaders work with executive management to establish a network that includes every line manager. Their concept is that business unit managers have the ultimate stake in performance improvement. They believe the internal partner network only becomes viable when line and staff managers understand that their success depends on working together with the HPI department in improving performance.

The creation and implementation of the HPI network is built on preparing an action plan that is jointly developed and supported by the CEO, senior management, and the HPI leader and practitioners. The plan serves as a guide to identifying potential partners and securing the necessary commitment for joint HPI actions and sharing of resources. Table 4-2 contains some steps and tasks to consider in building a plan for your organization.

The internal partners listed in table 4-3 are found in many organizations. Common goals, such as service quality, employee satisfaction, and customer satisfaction, are only accomplished when the entire organization is focused on working together to accomplish these goals. Using the resources and expertise of these internal partners often saves the performance consultant time, a great deal of expense, and helps the client receive the best possible performance support.

Creating External Alliances

Alliances created outside of the organization are a particularly valuable source of resources and support for the HPI department. Several organizations share a common mission of improving performance. The opportunity lies in understanding the purpose and goals of each of these organizations listed in table 4-4 and how they align with the performance improvement goals of the HPI department. With the support of key individuals within your organization who have ties to these potential partners, the HPI leader

Table 4-2: Develop a plan for creating an HPI network and alliances.

Planning Step	Task
Identify benefits of the HPI network and external alliances.	List benefits for each service partner and extended alliance partner.
Conduct an assessment of performance support and resources.	Identify resource gaps for critical performance support needs.
Identify potential internal service partners and external alliance partners.	Establish a selection process and criteria.
Gain and maintain CEO and executive management support.	Communicate the benefits and successes of internal HPI network and external alliances.
Set expectations within the organization on HPI network and external alliances.	Manage expectations by underpromising and overdelivering results.
Implement contracts with internal and external partners.	Outline the operating standards, policies, procedures, measures, and agreements for establishing partnerships.
Measure and communicate early successes.	Develop a performance scorecard and communication strategy.
Reward and recognize successes.	Develop a reward and recognition process.
Maintain internal and external partnerships.	Hold frequent meetings, communicate, and reward successes.

and practitioners can use the sales and service skills of relationship managers to plan and conduct an initial meeting (chapter 7).

One important issue faced by every HPI leader is how to balance the competing demands of heavy existing commitments with the time to learn and apply the HPI process. This dilemma is helped through external alliances. Each external organization and agency listed in table 4-4 has a mission to improve the skills, knowledge, and occupational well-being of the citizens they serve. Each has resources in people, facilities, and equipment that are well worth the effort of establishing formal partnerships. The agreement establishing the formal partnership is often documented in a memorandum of understanding or contract that is signed by the HPI leader or the CEO. The contract outlines the purpose of the partnership, standards and goals, communication, sharing of products, services, and best practices, joint interventions, measurement, and pricing.

GOVERNMENT AGENCIES. The federal government has a vital interest in a highly skilled, knowledgeable, technically proficient, educated, and critical-thinking citizenry for the future well-being of the nation. Agencies within

Table 4-3. The HPI partner network.

Internal Partner Network	Support for HPI
Audit	• shares information on underperforming business units and performance problems • assists in root-cause analysis and in identifying actions to improve performance
Facilities	• provides space for meetings, focus groups, training, and offices for the HPI department
Finance	• creates and models HPI scorecard financial measures • assists with financial data analysis
Line and Staff Managers	• serve as subject matter experts and facilitators of refresher training on-the-job • evaluate field testing of new HPI products and services • partner with HPI practitioners • communicate HPI capabilities and projects
Market Research	• provides assessment data for the performance consultant through data collection and benchmark surveys, facilitating focus groups, sorting and analyzing data, and creating reports
Public Relations	• prepares communication and marketing strategy for promoting the HPI department • helps performance consultants with scripting client meetings and educating the organization on HPI products, services, and benefits

the government, obviously the U.S. Department of Education, support educational excellence through grants and support to the states. There are other agencies, most notably the U.S. Department of Defense, that have invested heavily in performance consulting, innovative uses of technology, leadership development, and standards of excellence in training and education. The U.S. Department of Agriculture offers graduate programs *par excellence* in myriad subjects including leadership, training, business, and even foreign language with an emphasis on business communication.

Partnering with local divisions of these agencies on joint initiatives, sharing of facilities, and best practices can be very beneficial.

Several state governments are following the lead of such progressive states as North Carolina and Texas in establishing partnerships between business and government in support of education. This focus involves improving K–12 standards in curriculum, testing, and outcomes. Business leaders and HPI practitioners provide recommendations on quality and

Table 4-4. Potential external alliance partners.

Potential External Alliance Partners	Potential Support Provided to HPI Department
Government Agencies	• government, education, and business partnering on education and skills of K–12 and college students for employability • grants for specific training and education projects • shared resources for joint initiatives that may include consulting team members, facilities, and equipment
Universities and Colleges	• programs on executive and leadership development, research, and knowledge management • faculty consultations in strategic planning • faculty and professional specialists for consulting teams, process facilitators, coaches, and mentors
Community Colleges	• programs on basic and occupational skills, PC and Internet skills, training in sales and service, leadership development, and basic business principles • facilities and equipment
Professional Associations	• technical and consulting competencies, development, and certification offerings • research expertise available • report preparation and distribution • accessibility to data through Website
Noncompetitor Peer Organizations	• joint consulting initiatives, training, and projects • data sharing on best practices • facilities and equipment

performance improvement principles as part of a school district quality committee chaired by the school superintendent. The Malcolm Baldridge Award (National Institute of Standards and Technology, 1987) is used as an objective standard to drive qualitative improvements in primary, secondary, higher, and occupational education. The opportunity for the HPI department lies in establishing a partnership that allows the sharing of data, models, and solutions with public agencies on common performance problems. These performance problems, for example, may involve literacy, management, cultural diversity, and retention. Another benefit is that the Baldridge model and quality principles may be taught to the HPI department's practitioners by esteemed professionals in government agencies.

INSTITUTIONS OF HIGHER EDUCATION. Universities, colleges, and community colleges have a mission to support the educational and occupational needs of the citizenry they serve. Partnerships with colleges and universities offer a number of opportunities to shift the burden of high volume, generic training from the HPI department to the college. They have faculty, facilities, and equipment that may be available to support skills and knowledge improvement initiatives within the organization. Often faculty members have background in quality, organizational development, measurement, and evaluation. Faculty can facilitate workshops for the HPI staff and serve on consulting teams, freeing up resources for the HPI leader to build and implement the new HPI process and department. A higher education alliance can provide the HPI department with a source of reasonably priced, high-quality performance support.

PROFESSIONAL ASSOCIATIONS. Appendix C lists some of the many professional associations that have a mission related to performance improvement. Several of them are actively pursuing HPI practitioners as members and as customers for their products and services. As these professional associations continue to operate more as businesses than as traditional nonprofit membership organizations, the competition among them accelerates. From the HPI practitioner's point of view, it often appears that they must belong to up to four or five different associations to get the full professional support they need.

The HPI profession cuts across any number of professional and membership associations, but none of these associations has taken the lead in becoming the home for the expanded family of HPI practitioners advocated by this book. What the HPI profession needs is less competition and more cooperation among professional associations. As HPI practitioners need to rally around one HPI process, the professional associations need to focus on the performance needs of their members. This will lead to the integration of their processes and tools into a comprehensive, unified approach to performance improvement.

For these actions to occur, several of the larger associations will have to come together in the interests of the profession and their membership by building bridges around joint initiatives and common interests. These initiatives may involve task forces comprising staff and members to create common terms, concepts, models, and developmental approaches to HPI. It may also mean joint ventures in dual membership, multisponsored conferences, and reliance upon the products and services of several professional associations. All these activities may lead to a global consortium of associations formed around the common theme of serving the HPI community.

To do all of this will take many years and the combined efforts of two constituencies in the HPI profession. Practitioners must demand that the associations to which they belong take ownership for the changes in professional support of HPI outlined in *Building a New Performance Vision*. They must require the elimination of competition among associations and a renewed focus on the performance needs of members. A leader or several leaders of larger associations must have the vision and conviction to respond to the demand for action and lead the change process.

NONCOMPETITOR PEER ORGANIZATIONS. Another opportunity for creating external alliances is in the HPI departments from noncompeting organizations working together on common performance problems. This collaboration may involve jointly developing and delivering training, sharing facilities, and working together on common HPI interventions. Often these joint interventions involve improving service quality to internal and external clients, leadership development programs, or systems implementation. A council of HPI leaders is sometimes formed to formalize long-term collaboration on performance support. Resources are pooled, joint activities are implemented, data is collected and shared, and results are measured. The council can meet periodically to plan joint ventures, review progress, and develop communications on successes.

Consulting teams with participants from several organizations work well when there is agreement on the use of a common HPI process. Effective partnerships with external organizations require consensus on the working tools used by consultants for client interventions. This must be a nonnegotiable working agreement or clause in the collaboration contract. Otherwise, practitioners and clients spend more time trying to reconcile inconsistencies in language, process models, and tools than actually improving performance.

OVERCOMING BARRIERS TO SUCCESS AND LESSONS LEARNED. Table 4-5 lists some lessons learned in establishing and maintaining successful relationships between HPI departments and institutions of higher education, government agencies, professional associations, and noncompeting organizations in the marketplace.

Action Step 4: Measure, Communicate, and Celebrate Successes

Use a scorecard (chapter 10) with balanced measures to determine the value of internal network and external alliance partner collaboration. Agree on the approach to measurement and specific metrics early in the planning of a joint activity. You may need to conduct minisessions on the HPI process and performance scorecard to educate team members who are from functions outside the HPI department. This is essential to ensure that the team has a common understanding of the process, tools, and terms for joint projects. It is

Table 4-5. Implementing successful alliances.

Barrier to Successful Alliances	Lesson Learned in Overcoming Barrier
Senior managers are reluctant to enter into external alliances or build an internal HPI network.	Educate senior management on the benefits of the alliance and the internal gaps in HPI resources and capabilities required to support the business.
The network or alliance fails to achieve expected results because of participation issues.	Gain and maintain the commitment of senior management to allow employees the time to attend activities that support a business or performance need.
Partners are disappointed with the waste of resources in preparing activities that do not meet expectations because of inflated estimates of need and attendance.	Estimate conservatively the number of employees who will attend jointly sponsored programs.
External and internal partners fail to meet expectations in the quality of products and services delivered.	Orient partners on the vision, values, and strategic direction of the organization and HPI department. For each activity, jointly prepare and conduct the first few sessions to ensure appropriate quality in design, content, and delivery.
The dedication of appropriate resources, skilled staff, and quality of activity falls short of contracted standards.	Carefully outline and reach consensus on standards and performance objectives for jointly sponsored activities. Review standards as part of each activity preparation session.
Employees are unable to attend activities because of the lack of timely notification.	Establish procedures on employee selection, scheduling, notification of acceptance, and reporting instructions for each activity.
Senior management support for network and alliance resources is jeopardized by competing demands.	Keep the senior management team in the loop on all developments, successes, and issues. They must feel a sense of ownership.

important to be sensitive to using performance measures that have credibility in the organizations collaborating on the joint activity.

Effective communication is coordinated with each partner to jointly develop talking points for management briefings, HPI department meetings, and enterprise public relations. Give credit for participation, best practices, and results to demonstrate the mutual benefits realized through the HPI network and alliances. Celebrate successes through awards, dinners, and communications targeted to the recipient's organization.

Progress Milestones

This chapter gave you a good background in how to create the networks and alliances that will make the next step in the process much easier. Establishing internal networks and external alliances can mean the difference between success and failure in the resource-constrained environment of most HPI departments. Structure must enhance capability so that the sum of the parts is greater than the whole. This is often particularly true in attempting to integrate HPI functions and operate effectively in a shared-services environment. The opportunities for the HPI department, the internal network partners, and external alliance partners are only limited by your willingness to think outside of the box and take risks. The basis for any successful external alliance is the same as for internal client partnerships—a strong working relationship based on mutual trust and support.

Key Points of This Chapter

✔ Link benefits to participating in the network and alliances to specific results for each stakeholder.

✔ Select potential partners based on similarities in culture, values, performance problems, processes, tools, and the availability and willingness to dedicate resources for joint HPI initiatives.

✔ Document operating agreements, standards, policies, and procedures in a contract signed by each partner.

✔ Anticipate barriers to success in implementing the network and alliances, and develop specific actions to surmount each potential barrier.

✔ Measure results using a jointly developed scorecard, generously recognize the achievements of your partners, and communicate these results.

Rallying the Organization, Building the Process

This chapter focuses on an approach to developing a common process for your HPI department. A sample of the process models currently used in the marketplace is reviewed as background for you to reflect on the components of each model and their applicability to your organization. A new HPI process is proposed from this review of process models and recommended as a starting point for you to use in your efforts to create a customized, integrated model for your HPI department. The approaches to building a new HPI process are presented as a case study. The steps that you may use to create an HPI process for your organization are as follows:

 Action Steps to Rally the Organization and to Create a Workable Process

1. Identify external HPI process models and internal HPI function models.
2. Determine whether to build or buy the process model.
3. Build a new HPI process customized for the needs of your organization.
4. Apply your knowledge to a case study.

The HPI leader is the performance improvement champion responsible for providing the leadership and vision needed to develop a new HPI process. The reality is that each HPI function often has its own process models, concepts, terminology, and tools. The practitioners in these functions likely believe their process model is the solution for client performance problems. Practitioners in these silos often do not have the process and competencies to completely support the client's business and performance needs. The result is that clients receive fragmented, good-faith efforts. This situation will not be resolved until processes, tools, and capabilities are integrated into a unified HPI vision.

Creating a common process is an early prerequisite for the successful integration of HPI functions. A process is a series of steps that help practitioners and clients work together to improve performance. The process includes phases and tools that help practitioners and clients identify performance problems, assess the root causes of performance gaps, agree on interventions, implement appropriate actions, and measure the impact of an intervention. The HPI team builds a process that supports the organization's strategic direction, culture, values, and business model.

Action Step 1: Identify External HPI Process Models and Internal HPI Function Models

Scores of process models in the marketplace representing the HPI functions are reviewed in this chapter. The purpose of this book is not to provide a detailed evaluation of the merits of these process models, but you should be aware of many of the models mentioned herein. Tables 5-1, 5-2, and 5-3 provide an overview of some of these process models and approaches to HPI. These tables list information on HPI functions with process models that are focused on skills and knowledge improvement, process improvement, and performance consulting. They are presented so that HPI leaders and practitioners can reflect on how to analyze process models and match the type of model needed to their organization's performance improvement needs. Practitioners with this knowledge are better positioned to successfully identify a model or components of several models that can be used in starting the process development effort. They can make well-informed decisions on whether to build or buy an HPI process.

Table 5-1 lists the skills and knowledge improvement functions. These functions focus on improving performance by creating learning organizations and increasing the on-the-job skills and knowledge of practitioners.

The industrial/organizational psychologists provide assessment, testing, and analytical support. They have valuable competencies in developing performance models that specify the selection criteria, performance expectations, and best practices for a position. Industrial psychologists measure employee attitudes on specific topics as well as employee satisfaction with the organization. They conduct organizational research, assess employee productivity, and design environmental changes to enhance performance.

The instructional systems design (ISD) function includes products and services dealing with workplace learning activities, formal and on-the-job training delivery, the design and development of instruction, and the sharing of information. Managers often provide on-the-job performance support by reinforcing formal learning through workplace skill refreshers, coaching, and the use of job aids and checklists. Formal learning activities often include classroom training and modular, self-paced, or video-based instruction.

Table 5-1. Skills and knowledge improvement functions.

Skills and Knowledge Functions	HPI Focus	Process Model
Industrial/Organizational Psychology	Conducts environmental testing, and skills and job analysis to identify the knowledge, skills, and support needed by employees to improve performance	There is no universally adopted process model.
Instructional Systems Design (Dick & Carey, 1996)	A systematic approach to the design of instruction. ISD includes learning initiatives needed to improve performance by increasing skills and knowledge	• identify instructional goals • conduct instructional analysis • identify entry behaviors • write performance objectives • develop criterion-referenced tests • develop instructional strategy • develop and select instruction • design and conduct formative evaluation • design and conduct summative evaluation • implement ISD and measure effect
Knowledge Management	Provides information and best practices by identifying, storing, and disseminating knowledge to improve individual and organizational performance	• manage databases • conduct research • develop policies and procedures • carry out competitor and industry intelligence

E-learning refers to any skills and knowledge delivered by electronic technology that is used to enhance learning. The capabilities include electronic performance support tools such as online referencing, Web-based learning, and computer-based training (CBT).

Knowledge management focuses on the accessibility to information that provides employees with best practices in improving on-the-job performance. Knowledge management is about institutionalizing methods for collecting the right information, managing the data, and providing ease of accessibility for sharing the organization's information resources. Information technology is needed in supporting Internet, intranet, and Web technologies for the electronic storage, classification, and retrieval of information. Knowledge management emphasizes using information to continuously improve performance on the job.

Although improving skills and knowledge is an important component of HPI, it is one set of actions in the HPI process model. Skills and knowledge actions must be fully integrated with process and performance consulting actions to provide clients with complete solutions and sustainable results. The process improvement functions (table 5-2) focus on analyzing and closing gaps in systems and work flows, policies, and procedures. The bottom-line effects of process improvement emanate from breakthroughs in performance achieved by increasing efficiency and productivity.

The IT function offers a system design methodology that supports usability testing of technology to ensure that it supports the performance expectations required of each position. Reengineering capabilities for existing systems offer the organization improved operational efficiencies through automation and elimination of manual processing. Systems support is provided for delivering HPI products and services that may be labor intensive or required at distant locations.

Table 5-2. Process improvement functions.

Process Improvement Function	HPI Focus	Process Model
Information Technology (IT)	Maximizes performance through the design and application of operational systems and the reengineering of business processes.	• Describe the project. • Identify vision, values, and objectives. • Analyze as-is status and gaps. • Design processes and tools. • Conduct benefit-cost analysis. • Develop implementation plan. • Implement the design. • Ensure continuous process improvement. • Measure results.
Strategic Planning	Analyzes and measures work tasks, procedures, and systems to improve operational efficiencies and productivity by implementing continuous improvement actions.	• Identify organization's strategic direction. • Identify organization and business unit goals. • Collect and analyze data on the marketplace, competitor's business model, products, and services, internal business results, and performance gaps. • Identify courses of action. • Implement and evaluate.
Total Quality Management (TQM)	Assesses, selects, and implements actions that establish an organization's strategic direction. Creates business models for improving results by enhancing effectiveness and efficiency.	• Identify current results. • Identify key clients and business needs. • Identify work-flow process steps. • Build measurement model. • Prioritize and implement actions. • Evaluate results.

The purpose of strategic planning is to serve as an internal change agent in improving the organization's business results. Strategic planning looks at the interface between the marketplace, the organization, and internal business units in developing the organization's strategic direction, organizational goals, and business unit objectives. This function assesses market and competitor capabilities, and compares these capabilities to that of the organization. Internal and external drivers of change and business unit size, growth, and goals are carefully analyzed. Business strategies and options are identified for the withdrawal, consolidation, or expansion of products, customer segments, and markets.

Total quality management provides a methodology for continuous improvement by changing procedures, systems, standards, costs, and results. This methodology involves working on total processes, looking for variations in results, and implementing solutions using the plan, do, study, act cycle (Deming, 1988). The quality function improves individual and business unit productivity by identifying inefficiencies in work flow, documentation, and systems support. Quality processes and changes in organizational culture often result in enhanced customer loyalty from improved service recovery, timely problem resolution, and problem prevention.

Table 5-3 lists four performance consulting related models that demonstrate the similarities and differences in processes. Organization development, HPT, and performance consulting define their value through change in organizational and performer results. Each stresses the alignment of process, organizational structure, performer readiness, strategy, and business needs. Each function strives for sustainable improvement in business and individual performance. Practitioners from each function are closely aligned in performance improvement values, beliefs, and approaches.

Subtle differences are noted in the way that OD, in practice, tends to place heavier emphasis on internal causes, whereas HPT and performance consulting balance internal and external causes in the work environment. Wile's (1996) cause analysis matrix is tremendously valuable in its systematic treatment of root causes and actions that close performance gaps. Performance consulting more strongly emphasizes partnering with clients as a fundamental prerequisite to successful performance improvement. Instead of being in competition with one another, practitioners from these functions should be natural allies in forming a new HPI process and department that mutually support the client.

There is probably no single model that can be taken off of the shelf and used effectively to solve every performance problem arising in today's complex, ever-changing organizations. The opportunity is for the HPI leader and practitioners to create a process with the flexibility and best practices of all of the HPI functions so that it is capable of evolving and adapting to the client's business needs.

Table 5-3. Performance consulting functions.

Performance Consulting Functions	HPI Focus	Process Model
Organizational Development (Cummins & Worley, 1998)	Maximizes performance through the design and application of operational systems and the reengineering of business processes.	• identify client • contract with client • analyze client's performance problems • build plan for implementing change • measure success • implement sustaining actions
Human Performance Technology (International Society for Performance Improvement, 1988)	A process of analysis, intervention selection, design, development, implementation, and evaluation, that most cost effectively influences human behavior and accomplishment	• performance analysis • cause analysis • intervention selection and design • implementation and change management • evaluation
Performance Consulting (Robinson & Robinson, 1998)	The science of improving human performance in the workplace through analysis and the design, selection, and implementation of appropriate interventions	• partnership • assessment • intervention actions • implementation and measurement • quality assurance
Cause Analysis Model (Wile, 1996)	An approach to the systematic analysis of root causes and appropriate actions that are integrated from the models of Gilbert, Harless, and Mager	• environmental causes: organizational systems and incentives • external resources: cognitive support, tools, physical environment • internal skills and knowledge • inherent ability of performers

Action Step 2: Build or Buy the Process Model

Now that you are aware of some of the existing models, you are ready to move beyond them and create an HPI process appropriate to the vision, values, strategic direction, and client needs of your organization. There are several approaches the HPI leader and practitioners may take in building an HPI process. They may decide to build the process internally because of the expertise of practitioners and sophistication of their function's models. Another approach is for the HPI leader to buy a model and the services of an external partner who guides practitioners through process development.

Building internally is often cost effective, fits the organization's strategy and culture, and enjoys strong practitioner ownership. There is often a great deal of time, expense, and frustration involved in the trial-and-error of internal process building. If an external partner is used, there is strong credibility in an expert who has successfully implemented an HPI process in a variety of organizations. Consulting fees and the expense of purchasing the rights to use a process are often more costly than building it from scratch. Some HPI leaders take the middle ground by purchasing the rights to use an existing model and customizing it through support from an external partner.

Whichever approach is used, the new HPI process must build on the successes of process models currently owned by practitioners in the organization. Each process model has its advocates and a history of results that serve as a testimonial to its effectiveness and worth. It is important to take this opportunity to unite practitioners around a new process that each has a role in creating. Overcoming entrenched loyalties often requires the objectivity and market credibility that an external partner with a proven process model brings to the organization.

Action Step 3: Build the New Process Model

Building the new process often starts with a series of planning meetings. The early objectives of these meetings are to

- ✦ ensure that all functions are involved in creating the new HPI process
- ✦ build an integrated process with a menu of tools and concepts that represent the best practices from each function
- ✦ gain early buy-in for the new process from clients and practitioners.

The ultimate objective is to build an HPI process model that clients will use for achieving their business needs. It must be a process that each practitioner will own and apply. The steps that are used by the cross-functional team in building the process are presented in table 5-4.

It is important to recognize that building an HPI process cannot be done with a cookie-cutter approach. Two organizations following the approach outlined in this book will almost certainly build different process models. This may be the result of differences in the organization's culture, strategic direction, and business models. It may also occur because of differences in the generic model and external partner selected, or the internal process models used by the HPI functions.

If the HPI leadership team decides to build the new process internally, then they may wish to use the model outlined in figure 5-1 as a starting point. This is an integrated HPI process synthesized from the function models listed in tables 5-1, 5-2, and 5-3.

The cross-functional consulting team develops a comprehensive list of the HPI functions, performance focus, and process models used by each

Table 5-4. Steps in building the new HPI process.

Steps	Actions
1. Form the leadership team.	The HPI leader, function managers, line champions(s), and external partner develop a high-level plan and goals, and create a contract agreeing to build a new process.
2. Conduct practitioner meetings.	The HPI leader conducts meetings to: • explain the need for an integrated HPI process • explain how the alignment of process with the vision, mission, values, structure, and performer readiness of the HPI department is critical to success • request the participation of all practitioners in the development and implementation of the new process • explain the benefits of a new process for the organization, the HPI department, and each practitioner.
3. Develop and implement a detailed plan.	The HPI leader, practitioners, and external partner prepare a timeline, tasks, and list of accountabilities for creating a new process.
4. Involve practitioners in design and development.	Practitioners are assigned to a cross-functional performance consulting team to: • design and develop phases of the new process from the best of the external partner's and HPI function's models • field test the conceptual design of each phase of the process with two or three clients.
5. Prepare the draft process model.	• A client partners with the team on a quick-turnaround, limited-scope performance problem. • All phases of the draft model are tested and carefully evaluated. • The leadership team reviews the consulting team's pilot results. • The team prepares a process draft.
6. Seek feedback and commitment.	• The HPI leader, key clients, and practitioners meet to get feedback, recommendations, and buy-in.
7. Implement the new process.	• Build the process support required for successful implementation. • Develop a performance consulting competency model • Develop new roles, job titles, and job descriptions (appendix B). • Develop learning actions that include a performance consulting workshop for practitioners to learn new competencies and the process model (chapter 6). • Test and continuously improve the process model based on client performance improvement interventions.

function in the organization. The functions outlined in tables 5-1, 5-2, and 5-3 are used as a checklist to ensure that all functions are included. The steps outlined in table 5-4 are appropriate for the team to follow. The detailed actions are adjusted for building the process internally. The team analyzes each process model by asking the following types of questions:

+ How does each model contribute to solving the client's performance problems?
+ What core concepts do all the process models have in common?
+ What is unique to each process model that needs to be preserved for a rich diversity of concepts and tools?
+ Is the model adaptable to integrating new concepts, tools, and terminology from each HPI function?
+ How is a menu of tools developed to represent the best of the HPI function models?
+ Who needs to be involved in finalizing decisions?
+ Is the new process aligned with the organization's vision, values, and strategy?
+ Are success measures in place to evaluate the effect of the HPI process on business results?

When completing this analysis of functions, the team will often find that assessment, identification of interventions, implementation of interventions, and measurement are found in virtually all of the process models. These are the components of the new process that often are easiest for practitioners from various HPI functions to quickly rally around. It is useful to start with agreement on these phases as early wins in building a core process. Terms, process steps, and tools are often issues that need to be negotiated.

The HPI process model in figure 5-1 establishes partnering and contracting as the foundation of the process. It acknowledges the reality that not all requests for support or proactive identification of performance problems are appropriate as consulting interventions and that there are ways of exiting the process with the client. The process builds on Wile's cause analysis matrix (Wile, 1996) and systematically assesses internal and external root causes.

Intervention actions are identified, and a menu of products, services, and tools are created to close performance gaps generated in the assessment phase. Intervention actions are prioritized in the implementation phase following Gilbert's (1996) belief that changes in the work environment are conducted prior to investing resources in skills and knowledge solutions. This approach saves the HPI department a great deal of time and expense because many consultants have found that up to 80 percent of the causes for performance problems are in the work environment. It also makes sense to have

Figure 5-1. HPI process model.

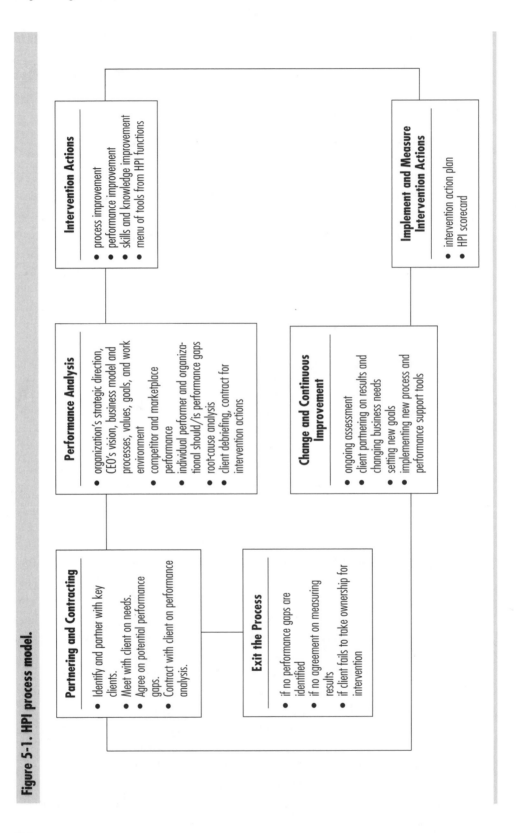

Partnering and Contracting

- Identify and partner with key clients.
- Meet with client on needs.
- Agree on potential performance gaps.
- Contract with client on performance analysis.

Exit the Process

- if no performance gaps are identified
- if no agreement on measuring results
- if client fails to take ownership for intervention

Performance Analysis

- organization's strategic direction, CEO's vision, business model and processes, values, goals, and work environment
- competitor and marketplace performance
- individual performer and organizational should/'s performance gaps
- root-cause analysis
- client debriefing, contract for intervention actions

Change and Continuous Improvement

- ongoing assessment
- client partnering on results and changing business needs
- setting new goals
- implementing new process and performance support tools

Intervention Actions

- process improvement
- performance improvement
- skills and knowledge improvement
- menu of tools from HPI functions

Implement and Measure Intervention Actions

- intervention action plan
- HPI scorecard

tools and systems in place so that the skills and knowledge improvement actions are aligned. An HPI scorecard is developed (chapter 10) that provides for the comprehensive measurement of process, performance consulting, and skills and knowledge improvement actions of interventions. Quality principles are applied in the continuous improvement of partnering skills, assessment methods, intervention actions, and scorecard measures.

What are the benefits of using this new HPI process?

+ There is greater emphasis on partnering with the client and contracting for actions to improve performance.
+ A richer treatment is provided for internal and external analysis of causes that influence performance.
+ There is a stronger array of intervention actions available to consultants for complete performance support to clients.
+ There is greater diversity and depth of tools available to consultants. The tools represent best practices from the HPI functions.
+ An HPI scorecard of measures with greater sophistication of quantitative and qualitative metrics is available to performance consultants and clients.
+ Longer-term results are sustained through continuous improvement actions as part of the intervention plan.

Another option is to use the OD model (table 5-3). This approach is feasible if the OD department has practitioners with strong consulting and design competencies, influence with key clients, and credibility within the organization. The OD process is often one of the strongest HPI function models in the organization and is designed with phases, tools, and concepts that provide a starting point for joint action by the cross-functional team. Instructional systems designers, OD specialists, and quality practitioners on the cross-functional team often have the competencies and tools to take strong leadership and process development roles on the consulting team. These practitioners provide the competencies and serve in consulting roles that are provided by the external partner when the decision is to buy and customize.

Action Step 4: Apply Your Knowledge to a Case Study

 Linda, the HPI leader of a high-tech company, and her practitioners determine that it is prudent to find an external partner and customize that partner's model to the needs of the organization. They decide that they do not have the internal expertise to build a process and support the existing demands of clients for support. How will Linda and the HPI practitioners decide which model and external partner to select? The following approach is one way to proceed in making this critical decision.

Linda recruits a cross-functional team of practitioners representing the HPI functions to carefully review the literature, attend conferences, and scan the marketplace for a process and external partner that is a good fit with the HPI department. While doing this research, they develop criteria to select an external partner and model. These criteria include the following:

+ The external partner has a track record of success in implementing the HPI model with peer high-tech organizations.
+ The external partner's model is aligned with the business model and values of the organization.
+ The external partner displays an understanding and commitment to the HPI department's vision.
+ The external partner's consulting style and interpersonal behaviors complement those of the HPI practitioners and clients.
+ The core design of the external partner's model can potentially serve as an integration umbrella for the HPI function's processes into the new HPI department.
+ The core design of the model is not overly complex, it can be customized with ease to the needs of the HPI department, and it can be learned and applied by practitioners.
+ The external partner commits the time to provide adequate support for building and implementing the new process.
+ The anticipated expenses of the external partner's service and the use of the model are within the department's budget parameters.

The cross-functional selection team sends a request for proposals to external partners identified through the research of the consulting team. The potential candidates are asked to provide the following information:

+ a list of clients who have created and implemented an HPI process using the candidates' model and consulting expertise
+ a sample of the implementation plan, actions, and tools used in an HPI client intervention
+ a detailed description of the candidate's process model
+ a detailed description of the candidate's HPI competency and measurement models
+ a description of the candidate's approach to working with the HPI department to customize the process
+ an initial estimate of expense.

After evaluating the proposals against the selection criteria, the cross-functional team narrows the list to three candidates. A panel interview is scheduled with cross-functional team and individual interviews with Linda and the HPI managers. Susan, a key client from one of the business divisions, is invited to participate in the interview process.

The interviews are performance-based and provide candidates with a performance problem scenario the HPI department is currently facing. The selection criteria are tested against each candidate's presentation and the responses to questions during the interviews. The cross-functional team meets with a neutral facilitator to review the candidate presentations and selection criteria. The candidates are rank-ordered, and a vote of confidence is taken on the acceptability of the number one candidate. With team consensus and Linda's approval, the external partner is retained and introduced to the HPI department.

Progress Milestones

This chapter showed you how to rally the organization and build a new HPI process based in part on the work of others but customized to fit the needs of your own organization. Build or buy, there is no right answer. Whichever route you decide to take, the full involvement of practitioners and clients in building, testing, and implementing the process is essential to the success of the HPI department. With the new process operational, the HPI department has a starting point for launching a new beginning in client performance support. The full capabilities of the HPI functions are now integrated and focused on complete solutions to client performance gaps.

Your ability as a new performance consultant to use the HPI process effectively with clients depends largely on your relationship with the client. Without effectively implementing the partnering and contracting phase of the process, the quality and completeness of the new HPI process are largely irrelevant. The new process model often becomes just another attractive binder that adorns a bookshelf.

With the organizational structure and process in place, the final piece of the alignment puzzle—practitioner readiness for applying the process on client interventions—must be designed and implemented. Chapter 6 ("Changing Practitioner Skills and Knowledge") presents several approaches to investing in creating competency models, formal workshops, and workplace development opportunities for the new consulting roles of your HPI practitioners.

The following key points are presented for your consideration in building a new HPI process for your organization.

Key Points in This Chapter

✔ Build a partnership of key clients, HPI practitioners, and executive management around the need for and benefits of creating a new HPI process.

✔ Involve all stakeholders in a leadership team to build an action plan for designing and developing the HPI process.

✔ Conduct an environmental scan of internal and external process models, identify the current process model capabilities that fit the needs of your organization, and agree on the gap.

✔ Involve as many practitioners as possible in the cross-functional teams that are developing the new HPI process.

✔ Build each phase of the model and test it. Pilot the complete model on a low-risk intervention with a trusted client. Be sure to share lessons learned with all stakeholders.

✔ Start applying the model with clients in quick-turnaround interventions. Be sure to manage client expectations by underpromising and overdelivering on results.

✔ Use the new process model to build a competency model and performance consulting workshop as the core learning vehicles for the HPI department.

Changing Practitioner Skills and Knowledge

One of the most difficult issues you will face as an individual practitioner or HPI leader is in personally letting go of the past, breaking out of self imposed silos, embracing new roles, new competencies, and a new HPI process. This chapter presents an approach that you as the HPI leader or as a practitioner may use to make the change to performing new roles in the HPI department. It also presents examples of the formal and on-the-job preparation needed by practitioners to achieve expectations for these new performance improvement jobs and roles. The steps you may want to follow in changing practitioner competencies in your organization are listed below.

❗ Action Steps to Change Practitioner Skills and Knowledge

1. The HPI leader identifies jobs, roles, and critical competencies.
2. Make assignment decisions with practitioners based on the "should/is" gap in competencies and capabilities for each HPI practitioner. Collect the data needed to build a plan for changing the competencies of practitioners.
3. Build workshops and workplace learning opportunities in collaboration with an external partner.
4. Create a supportive HPI work environment where time and resources are available for practitioners to learn new roles and competencies.

Action Step 1: Identify Jobs, Roles, and Critical Competencies

The job of performance consultant usually involves a number of different roles. A job is a permanent assignment of duties in a designated team or department. A role is an additional duty, either as part of a temporary or standing team. In small departments, individuals by necessity are expected to perform several transactional roles and process-focused roles. For example, the HR specialist with the job of recruiting 10 employees monthly may also be assigned a role of data analyst on the consulting team. The analyst sorts, creates storyboards, and summarizes survey data. In larger departments, resources are often available that permit the assignment of practitioners to full-time performance consulting jobs.

The HPI leader is responsible for implementing an approach to assigning and developing practitioner jobs and roles in the new HPI department. In many organizations, probably fewer than 20 percent of the practitioners in the new department have the competencies, experience, and willingness to be a senior performance consultant. The gap in competencies for new consulting roles is such that every practitioner will have new competencies to learn as part of the change to performance consulting.

In determining how to proceed, it is useful for the HPI leader and practitioners to create a list of data and information needed in defining jobs and roles for each practitioner. The HPI leader must gather such information to allocate scarce resources in building learning and nonlearning actions that help each practitioner gain and apply the consulting competencies appropriate to their new roles. Some of the data that is needed includes:

◆ Why does each practitioner need to change? How will the change benefit each practitioner?
◆ What does a performance consultant do that is different from the duties currently performed by the practitioner?
◆ How will the performance expectations change in performing this new job? How will progress toward goals be evaluated?
◆ What does each practitioner need to know to be successful?
◆ What kind of development and on-the-job support can each practitioner expect from the organization?

The HPI leader and practitioners need to determine which consulting roles are initially needed to support the business and performance needs of clients. This configuration will vary by organization depending on the size of the organization, the number of positions allocated to the HPI department, its mission and purpose, and specific priorities established for the department. Table 6-1 lists a number of jobs often found in HPI functions and the performance consulting roles that practitioners in these jobs are sometimes assigned.

Action Step 2: Make Assignment Decisions

The assignment decision on jobs and roles is based on several factors. The performance needs (based on client needs) of the new HPI department dictate

Table 6-1. Performance consulting major roles.

Former Job in Functional Silo	New Role in Unified HPI Department	Primary Duties
Classroom facilitator	Process facilitator	Conducts meetings with clients and team members to achieve specific outcomes
Training developer	Technologist	Designs and develops alternative delivery methods using host, PC, and Web technology in support of consulting interventions
Training developer	Survey designer	Prepares data collection tools and methods required for HPI interventions
HR employment specialist	Interviewer and information gatherer	Conducts surveys in person or by telephone, collects data through benchmarking and other research
OD specialist	Relationship manager	Partners with clients to assess needs, determines opportunities for HPI client support, and brokers HPI resources with clients
Quality specialist	Senior performance consultant	Possesses the experience and competencies to perform all phases of the HPI process
OD team leader	Consulting team leader	Possesses the experience and competencies to lead HPI consulting teams
Training manager	Coach	Provides facilitation and mentoring with less skilled consultants
HR information system specialist	Evaluator	Is responsible for the design and implementation of measurement strategies and tools using the HPI scorecard
IT specialist	Data analyst	Sorts, analyzes, and summarizes data for consulting interventions

the consulting jobs and roles to be performed. The manager reviews the performance consulting assignments with practitioners. The practitioner's previous assignments and experience are identified in the competency assessment and considered by the practitioner and manager when reaching a mutual decision. Anticipate resistance and anxiety from a number of practitioners as they think about the amount of change expected by the HPI leader.

Frequently communicate and reinforce the need and benefits of change to ease practitioner fears and gain buy-in. This involvement may remove some of the barriers for practitioners to learn and implement the new process. If there is an impasse on the consulting assignment, then the manager's judgment prevails. In a year, after learning and applying competencies in this new role, business needs may be reexamined and a change in role closer to the preference of the practitioner assigned.

When positions are assigned to each practitioner, development actions are identified and implemented as part of a development plan. Learning and workplace developmental actions are planned to gain and apply the skills necessary in becoming a performance consultant. Both types of actions should mutually support and benefit each practitioner's development. Learning actions are formal development opportunities that may involve attending an internal or external consulting workshop, college courses, conferences, or seminars. Workplace actions often include assignment to a consulting team, coaching, and the sharing of best practices. The HPI leader plans and budgets for departmentwide formal preparation of competencies where large numbers of practitioners have common developmental needs.

Action Step 3: Build Workshops and Workplace Learning Opportunities

The practitioners in the new HPI department will need to develop new performance consultant and specialty competencies that will require attending one or more formal workshops. These formal learning opportunities often include an HPI workshop, measurement workshop, relationship manager workshop, and the internal conference. Applications of these competencies are provided for in workplace development practices, such as the assignment to a performance consulting team, coaching, and the use of performance consulting tools. It is the combination of formal and workplace development activities that offers the practitioner the best opportunity for gaining new HPI competencies.

Human Performance Improvement Workshops

Each new practitioner is required to attend an HPI workshop. The HPI leader emphasizes that this is an opportunity for practitioners to improve competencies, and learn the new process while sharing expertise from their previous HPI functions. This workshop is ideally scheduled within 3 to 6 months of the practitioner's entry into the department. Attending this workshop starts the practitioner's personal journey to learning the HPI process, the basics of the HPI scorecard, and the consulting competency model.

The HPI workshop may be offered by the department's external partner or by a professional association—ASTD or the International Society for Performance Improvement (ISPI), for example. Workshops conducted by an association are most cost-effective. Using an external partner is more expensive but offers advantages in customizing the workshop to the vision, values, strategic direction, and business-unique needs of the organization. Regardless of the approach used, it is important that the workshop facilitator be an experienced performance consultant with expertise in customizing processes and implementing client interventions.

Experienced consultants should also assist the performance consulting workshop facilitator as coaches. Practitioners with competencies and experience in OD, ISD, and TQM are a source of potential coaches. Each workshop coach is assigned up to four or five participants. The external partner may provide coaches if internal practitioners are not available. These internal or external coaches provide the HPI practitioners with in-depth, skill-building opportunities. A competency log is maintained by each coach throughout the workshop to document each practitioner's progress in competency attainment. Practitioners are expected to come to the workshop with a consulting intervention in mind that they can work through the new HPI process.

One of the last activities of the workshop is creating an action plan to apply what has been learned. The coach meets with each new performance consultant to debrief the competency log, revise the development planning form by noting skill/knowledge improvements, and additional development opportunities recommended by the coach. The new performance consultant is expected to schedule frequent manager meetings to receive coaching on skills learned on the job and in the workshops. This is a valuable opportunity for the consultant and their manager to discuss how they will apply these skills and lessons learned.

Table 6-2 illustrates one approach to the design and content of an HPI workshop. The workshop includes skill-building exercises, group feedback discussions, coaching, and skill log reviews. The design and approach of the workshop is customized to the business and performance needs of the HPI department.

Performance Consulting Specialty Workshops

The HPI leader may find that preparation in addition to the HPI workshop is required for consultants with specialized roles and new competencies. These roles may include, for example, evaluator or relationship manager. Learning and applying the competencies required for these roles dictates additional training followed by practice and coaching on the job. The HPI

Table 6-2. Human performance improvement workshop agenda.

Workshop Topic	Content
Prework	• identify performance problem to be used in the workshop as a real case study for the HPI process • reading assignments on the history of HPI, terminology, and expectations on workshop performance by the HPI leader
Day One	
Welcome, Review of Objectives, and Agenda	• purpose and objectives of the workshop • review of workshop agenda • introductions and housekeeping details • HPI leader comments
Roles and Competencies	• various performance consulting roles in the HPI department • competencies required for success in each role • development process for gaining required skills
Partnering and Contracting	• proactive versus reactive partnering • planning and conducting the initial meeting • identifying potential performance gaps • developing and selling the contract to conduct an assessment of root causes
Day Two	
Assessment	• planning and identifying data collection sources and methods • tools for sorting and analyzing the data • storyboarding the data • preparing the data collection report • preparing for presentation of data with the client • presenting trends with objectivity • obtaining client agreement on root causes and appropriate actions • contracting to build intervention actions
Day Three	
Intervention Actions	• four categories of intervention actions • linking actions to root causes • design and development of actions • client review of actions and approval of intervention plan
Day Four	
Implementation and Measurement	• project management for consulting interventions • selection of intervention consulting team • client meetings and communication • use of HPI scorecard measures • HPI intervention case study
Continuous Improvement	• lessons learned and best practices • periodic mini-assessments of performance gaps • redesign actions
Summary and Adjournment	• update development plan and top three actions • review consulting team assignments

leader may be faced with outsourcing or developing internally these workshops. Several companies, universities, and associations offer programs on measurement for evaluators and the sales and service skills needed by new relationship managers.

A word of caution is appropriate. If practitioners are sent to generic, external workshops, be sure to educate them on how their newly learned competencies link into the new HPI process. By sending them to these generic learning opportunities, the HPI leader may inadvertently promote the very silos that he or she is trying to eliminate. Practitioners may be introduced to models that do not reinforce the HPI department's process and total performance solutions.

HPI Scorecard Workshop

The objectives and content of the scorecard workshop are aligned with the HPI process and content presented in the HPI workshop. Developing and using the scorecard breaks down silos between functions in the HPI department and with clients. This workshop is strongly recommended for senior consultants, evaluators, analysts, team and sub-team leaders. Prerequisites to attend the workshop often include the following:

+ completion of the performance consulting (HPI) workshop
+ previous experience in measurement
+ analytical capabilities and skills to master using the scorecard with clients
+ willingness to specialize and learn new competencies for performing a measurement role.

Often it is a good idea to hire the one external partner to help build the HPI process and facilitate both the HPI workshop and the scorecard workshop. Several experienced coaches with in-depth expertise in the scorecard must be available during the workshop to mentor participants. Use internal consultants if possible but do not hesitate to use an external partner with necessary expertise. The ability of consultants to work with clients in measuring the success of HPI interventions hangs in the balance. This is no time to be miserly. The HPI leader needs to invest in the competencies of consultants in measurement roles and in creating and implementing the HPI scorecard.

No matter how unique the HPI department, process, or organization, certain core content is required for this workshop so that all will understand what the scorecard measures, their roles in using the scorecard, and how the scorecard integrates into and supports the phases of the HPI process. Furthermore, it is critical to establish sources and methods of data collection, analysis, and reporting. The workshop should also cover how to communicate with clients on the purpose, value, and need for the HPI scorecard.

The HPI leader and practitioners take every opportunity to educate clients on the need and benefits of using the HPI scorecard success measures. Communication opportunities involve discussing the scorecard at business unit meetings, articles in the organization's news, and presentations at organizational sales meetings. Integrating the HPI scorecard into leadership development programs is an opportunity to influence managers within the organization. It is important for line and staff managers outside of the HPI department to learn the basics of the scorecard model and how it supports their business goals. Clients also need to see the scorecard as a tool they can use within their business units to strengthen alignment with strategy and results. Using the scorecard strengthens the HPI department's credibility with business units by focusing consultants and clients on common performance measures.

Relationship Manager Workshop

The role of the relationship manager (RM) is essential to the success of the HPI department in implementing the new process and in supporting client needs. The RM workshop is another integration opportunity for HPI practitioners. The HPI leader selects RMs from each function in the HPI department. Because many HPI practitioners come from HPI functions that did not emphasize forming partnerships and building client relationships, a workshop is needed to provide a baseline of sales and service skills needed for success.

A most effective method for conducting the workshop is for a highly credible HPI function manager or senior performance consultant and line sales manager to facilitate the workshop together. The HPI consultant serving as facilitator needs prior sales and service line experience, strong consulting competencies, and group-process skills. The line manager provides client insight on the value of the relationship manager role, client expectations, and needs. The HPI consultant facilitates 95 percent of the workshop.

The prerequisites for attending the workshop include the following:

✦ completion of the HPI workshop
✦ basic knowledge of the client's business and sales and service models
✦ sales and service experience
✦ willingness to perform the role of relationship manager.

An example of the objectives and content of a relationship management workshop is listed in table 6-3. The design and content of the workshop are customized to the needs of the organization, clients, and relationship managers.

Table 6-3. Relationship manager (RM) workshop agenda (one day).

Workshop Topic	Content
Welcome, Review of Objectives and Agenda	• role of the RM • RM selection profile and required competencies • development process for gaining required skills • practice of critical sales and service skills
Role and Skills	• RM role, selection profile, skills • sales and service skills exercises • development plan and competencies
Skill-Building Exercises	• scheduling the initial meeting • preparing for the initial meeting • RM sales and service process • client follow-up
Relationship Manager Development	• update competency assessment for RM skills and knowledge • coaching • update development plan and top three actions
Summary and Adjournment	

Sales and service skills are often lacking in HPI practitioners. In recognition of this traditional skill gap, this section will provide detail about developing sales and service skills. Service quality skills and service standards are integrated throughout the workshop. The workshop uses the organization's generic sales and service process to teach RMs how to sell. All of these skills are discussed and practiced through case studies and role play.

The sales and service skills presented in the workshop include

✦ getting to know the client
✦ identifying the client's business and performance needs
✦ identifying an HPI benefit for each client need
✦ securing client agreement on implementing actions and client follow-up
✦ keeping good notes on the client (see appendix A).

GET TO KNOW THE CLIENT. When meeting the client for the first time, introduce yourself, shake hands, and thank the client for the meeting. Confirm the purpose of the meeting, and then work on getting to know the client as a person. Demonstrate interest in the client. Share some personal information or compliment the client on some recent achievement or event. Remember: The client's first impressions are formed within 60 seconds of the meeting.

IDENTIFY THE CLIENT'S NEEDS. Your ability as an RM to successfully implement HPI solutions depends on understanding the client's business needs. Ask questions and let the client talk about the business while you listen carefully and take notes. Questioning techniques involve asking open- and closed-ended questions, listening, and summarizing the client's needs.

Phrase open-ended questions to get the client to share as much information as possible. These questions usually begin with words such as *please explain, tell me, how, why,* and *describe.* Examples of open-ended questions are the following:

+ Tell me about how you have structured your division.
+ How do you think the organization is changing?
+ What are your goals for the next quarter?
+ How well are you currently achieving your goals?
+ What are the performance or leadership issues you have with your direct reports?

Closed-ended questions are phrased to get specific information or a *yes/no* type of client response. Closed-ended questions begin with words such as *how many, who, when, do you know,* and *will you.* Ask the client both open- and closed-ended questions. Closed-ended questions to clients may include:

+ When did you first recognize this performance gap?
+ How many of your employees are achieving expectations?
+ Who are your exemplary performers?
+ Are you willing to work in partnerhip with me to collect data on this performance gap?

IDENTIFY AN HPI BENEFIT FOR EACH NEED. It is the responsibility of relationship managers to help clients understand how the HPI department can support the business needs identified in this meeting. Do this, for example, by pointing out the following general benefits for clients working with the HPI department:

+ New models, tools, skills, and capabilities available through the new, unified HPI department offer the client new opportunities for achieving business goals.
+ The new HPI department is focused on supporting the success of the client rather than competing for client ownership.
+ The new HPI process guides the performance consultant to systematically approach clients on why performance problems are occurring and what can be done to improve their business results.

+ The HPI practitioners have a strong commitment to deliver products and services with a quality that delights the client.
+ The client's RM coordinates the efficient delivery of HPI support and follows up on quality control.

SECURE THE CLIENT'S AGREEMENT. The RM's objective in the initial meeting is to reach agreement with the client about obtaining information or investigating a potential performance gap. The RM often transfers the client or the project to another performance consultant. The handoff may be to a consulting team leader or senior consultant with the competencies necessary to implement actions that will close the client's performance gaps. The RM briefs the consulting team leader on the client and the project using a client profile worksheet. Follow up with both the client and consulting team leader immediately after the team leader meets the client. Is the client satisfied? If not, help the client resolve any issues. Support the consulting team in living up to the client's expectations outlined in the contract.

KEEP GOOD NOTES ON THE CLIENT. Use the HPI client meeting summary worksheet (appendix A) to document what is learned in each client meeting. Immediately after each meeting, list the critical elements of information that other consultants need to know, and rapidly circulate the information as an email. After each meeting review the meeting summary, look for gaps in the information collected, and write down how it will be obtained. The meeting summary worksheet is a valuable tool for communicating with other relationship managers and HPI practitioners. When another RM is assigned to the client, he or she will not need to waste the client's time gathering information that has already been collected.

Other Formal Development Opportunities: The Internal Conference

Another formal learning action is for the HPI leader to conduct an internal conference, usually within a year of implementing the HPI workshop. This is an excellent opportunity for the more experienced practitioners from the HPI functions to share specialized models, concepts, scorecard measures, and tools. It also provides a forum for sharing early successes and lessons learned in implementing the newly learned HPI process, relationship management techniques, the HPI scorecard, and consulting competency model. The conference is another opportunity for newly trained performance consultants to celebrate early wins. The internal conference builds teamwork, emphasizes progress in breaking down silos, and reinforces the department's primary focus on the client's business needs.

The agenda for this conference involves a celebratory dinner the first evening, with guest speakers, awards, and much humor. The conference should be scheduled for a minimum of 2 days. General sessions, which are attended by all, are held at the beginning and end of each day. The conference includes multiple breakout sessions, with practitioners selecting sessions that offer the best opportunity for learning and improving critical competencies. General sessions may involve presentations by senior line clients about their ongoing business needs, the value of performance consulting, and next steps for further improving performance support. Other presenters may be obtained from HPI-focused professional associations. Some of the breakout sessions should be assigned to senior practitioners within the new HPI department. They must have the expertise and credibility to further the competency development of large numbers of new performance consultants. External partners, local university faculty, the HPI leader, and function managers should also serve as breakout session presenters.

Each practitioner takes ownership for fully participating in every available learning and networking opportunity. For the HPI leader, the conference provides yet another forum for integrating the models, tools, and terminology of the HPI functions into the unified HPI process. This conference is an investment in the future of each practitioner and the new HPI department that should be planned as an annual developmental event.

Workplace Developmental Actions

Consultant development in the workplace is absolutely essential to gain depth of expertise in the performance consulting competencies and confidence in the new HPI process. After completing a workshop, the new consultant continues to develop on-the-job by applying what was learned with clients. The HPI leader sets the expectation that consultants are assigned to consulting teams and relationship managers assigned clients within 2 weeks of completing their training. Consultants with high levels of competency may begin working as lead performance consultants with the clients. Otherwise, it is probably best to work as part of a consulting team. This team assignment allows newly trained consultants to learn from more experienced consultants. By carefully selecting the first assignment, an early success can be achieved soon after completing the workshop. Workplace development actions also include the support of a coach, strong leadership, frequent communication, and the resources to support the expected performance of new consultants.

Coaching

After the time, effort, and money spent on the assessment and training of newly assigned consultants, how does the HPI leader ensure that practitioners use and further develop these competencies? This is a critical issue in transforming each function's process, tools, and terminology into the new, unified HPI process. It is the application of the new process and consulting competencies with clients that drives the integration of functions and practitioners into performance consultants. The role of the coach is critical for each practitioner's on-the-job learning and application of new competencies.

The role of the coach is separate from that of the manager with performance management responsibilities. Each coach serves as a workshop facilitator as well as a workplace mentor on performance consulting. Many new consultants feel more comfortable working with a peer coach rather than a manager when asking questions, getting advice, and admitting to what they don't know. The coaches cannot supplant the manager's role in performance counseling. Rather, the coaches are technical experts with depth of performance improvement skills and knowledge to share.

The coach is selected and specially prepared for the role of coach based on each individual's HPI expertise, business knowledge, and credibility as a consultant. The HPI leader selects at least one coach from each of the HPI functions. The few selected as coaches attend special preparation in a coach's workshop. After completing the workshop, they serve an apprenticeship as an assistant coach in a consulting workshop. Upon successfully completing the internship, each individual is assigned the role of coach. This small cadre of coaches also forms an internal "fire brigade" of excellent consulting team leaders and RMs.

All members of the HPI department receive informal coaching whenever the opportunity presents itself but not less than once monthly by a coach or manager. The informal coaching may be a brief inquiry about the status of a consulting team assignment, praise or words of encouragement, or recommended next steps. Formal coaching is required quarterly between each consultant and manager. This progress review involves a development plan update on competency target level attainment.

Performance Consulting Tools

What tools and resources will the HPI leader and the organization provide for the developmental support of each HPI practitioner in becoming a performance consultant? One important resource is a consulting guide. The guide is a binder containing best practices and lessons learned on each phase of the new HPI process. It serves as a consulting process road map with a series of job aids, checklists, and templates drawn from the various HPI functions and blended into the new HPI process. Each practitioner receives the guide at the beginning of the HPI workshop. It is used as a reference in the workshop and then used on the job as a resource in working on client interventions.

Sharing knowledge and lessons learned for immediate application is a valuable workplace development opportunity. Software programs accessed via an intranet are excellent tools for capturing and disseminating knowledge to other performance consultants working on similar interventions. This consulting knowledge management system also allows for timely communication on new consulting interventions, consulting team assignments, and benchmarking best practices. Less technology-dependent but effective knowledge management approaches are HPI department newsletters and monthly performance consultant brown-bag lunches.

Action Step 4: Create a Supportive HPI Work Environment

How can you find the time to do everything? Reconciling the time demands to learn and apply performance consulting may be a difficult problem for HPI practitioners and managers to work through, at least initially. The demands of supporting the current business reality appear overwhelming when trying also to carve out the time required for learning and applying new competencies with clients. Performance consulting interventions must be planned so that they do not add to existing workloads whenever possible. Performance consultants, with the help of coaches and managers, need to recognize that some of the administrative and performance activities they perform already support the HPI process. Integrating the new demands of the HPI process into the mainstream of daily activities must be the rule, not the exception.

Time is better managed by eliminating activities that are not supported by the results from business needs assessment. Conducting training because it is at the client's request or because it has always been the solution of choice can no longer become the default position. Eliminating training in these situations creates opportunities for higher-value use of your time and saves money for the organization, too. The HPI leader, managers, and performance consultants must be ruthless in the management of time. This is essential to balancing the change to performance consulting while always being attentive to the needs of clients and internal partners.

What motivates practitioners to want to change skills, knowledge, and behaviors? Strong leadership modeling consulting behaviors and leading by example are critical to success. Pride in the achievement of new skills and knowledge; recognition by peers, managers, and clients; and the opportunity for financial rewards motivate HPI practitioners to change and learn new competencies. The combination of well-planned financial and nonfinancial incentives is the most effective driver of change.

The nonfinancial incentives are often the least well understood drivers. They are effective, low-cost enhancers of behavior change. Awards of a company wristwatch, pen-and-pencil sets, and certificates of appreciation presented at a team meeting to worthy individuals are very effective motivators. The presentation must include a detailed description of the new consulting skills demonstrated by the new consultant and specific results achieved. A recognition column in the HPI department newsletter and time set aside at HPI meetings for recognizing consultant achievements are very effective. Recognition should be instituted as an ongoing tradition of inspiring excellence in consulting competency.

Financial motivators, such as bonuses and promotional opportunities, are based on demonstrating new competencies in client interventions. New jobs and roles, titles, job descriptions, and performance expectations require a flexible compensation system to reward increased value to the organization. As consultants demonstrate new competencies on the job with favorable results, the HPI leader needs the authority to increase pay without a change in position or title. A career-banding compensation system provides the manager with this flexibility. The issue here is that if the organization does not provide for the financial reward of those who gain new competencies and demonstrate increased value, then another organization will. The HPI leader owes it to the HPI department and the organization to carefully think through a performance consultant retention strategy. Otherwise, the HPI department becomes an excellent provider of consulting talent for the marketplace.

Progress Milestones

This chapter provides you with a perspective on the types of learning experiences that need to be planned and implemented to help practitioners make the transition to the new HPI process. In this chapter you have learned about the new HPI roles and competencies needed by practitioners and the decision-making process in making role assignments. The topics and content for a series of workshops and the application of these competencies in the work environment were presented as essential for the new HPI department to deliver complete performance support to clients.

The foundation has now been established for you to do an in-depth investigation on how to build the new HPI process and implement it effectively in your organization. This is the focus of part three of this book.

Key Points of This Chapter

✔ Encourage investment in time and resources to build a series of formal and workplace learning experiences that practitioners will need to make the transition to the new HPI process.

✔ Identify available resources and do an environmental scan to determine resource availability from potential internal partners and external alliances.

✔ Create a marketing and communication plan explaining why the change in process and competencies is necessary, how it can be done, and the benefits everyone in the HPI department will enjoy.

✔ Rotate the entire HPI team through these learning experiences. Everyone in the department needs to understand and be able to apply competencies appropriate for their role that supports the new HPI process.

✔ Implement the practitioner roles and skill-transition plan, measure early successes, learn from mistakes, and share lessons learned with clients and HPI practitioners.

 **PART THREE**

Improving Performance Through the HPI Process

This part of *Building a New Performance Vision* deals with the operational aspects of implementing the unified HPI process. Practical approaches, checklists, and case studies will help you to integrate the capabilities of the HPI functions and practitioners for mutual support of the client. In every situation, the emphasis is that these approaches are tools that you can use as a starting point for customizing them to your organization's strategic direction, business model, vision, and values. Take a look at the goals for this part. After reviewing this macro view of the phases of the HPI process, read each chapter for specific approaches and recommendations for applying each phase in your organization. Chapter 7 ("Partnering and Contracting") covers goals 1 and 2, chapter 8 ("Gathering and Assessing Data") captures goals 3 and 4, chapter 9 ("Implementing HPI Interventions") addresses goals 5 and 6, and chapter 10 ("Measuring HPI Success With the HPI Scorecard") speaks to goals 7 and 8.

Goals for Part Three

1. Develop the partnering and contracting phase of the HPI process with the cooperation of all of the HPI functions, key clients, and internal partners.
2. Establish the performance consulting role of the RM. Select and support the RMs in their roles of sales,

service, needs identification, and communication interface between the client and the HPI department.

3. Build and implement the data collection plan with a data collection team representing appropriate internal partners and evaluators from the various HPI functions.

4. Collect, analyze, summarize, and report the data to the client and agree on next steps as outlined in the consulting contract.

5. Build a cross-functional consulting team representing all of the HPI functions and providing complete performance solutions for the client.

6. Develop actions based on root-cause analysis and prepare an implementation plan for a successful intervention to improve performance.

7. Design, develop, and deliver an HPI scorecard that represents the best practices and tools from each HPI function.

8. Partner with key clients and internal partners in aligning HPI scorecard measures with business strategies and organizational metrics.

Partnering and Contracting

If the new process and department are built, will they come? The ultimate success of the new HPI department depends on the willingness of clients to work with you on their performance problems. Building a partnership that stands the test of time has as much to do with mutual trust and respect between you and the client as it does with the quality of the HPI department's process, products, and services. A partnership is about communicating openly, understanding the client's business needs, and contracting with the client on actions that support improved performance. A partnership, to be effective, involves a mutually beneficial focus on expectations, results, and opportunities for breakthroughs in performance. This chapter will explain how you can build and sustain partnerships with clients as the foundation for the future success of the HPI department.

 ## Action Steps to Successful Partnering and Contracting

1. Design the RM's role and operating procedures for maximum value to the client.
2. Identify potential RMs in collaboration with HPI managers. Interview and select RMs using the selection profile contained in the performance model.
3. Prepare a performance model for the RM to include role description, performance expectations, selection criteria, and success measures.
4. Build components for the partnering and contracting phase of the HPI process.
5. Provide for RM performance feedback through a client satisfaction survey.
6. Apply your knowledge to a case study.

Action Step 1: Design the RM's Role and Operating Procedures

Everyone within the HPI department is accountable for creating and sustaining client relationships. This presents a challenge for the HPI leader because some practitioners may have come from functions that were inwardly focused and operated in silos. Practitioners with a long history of working with process models and managers who do not emphasize partnership often find it difficult to change established patterns of behavior. The concept of partnership is often alien to individuals from this type of work environment. One approach to help practitioners focus on building and maintaining client relationships is to create the performance consulting role of RM.

The RM is the eyes and ears of the HPI department and communicates regularly with clients on current HPI initiatives and capabilities. The partnership between the RM and the client is strategic and tactical. Strategically, it involves partnering with clients on identifying organization-wide and business-unit opportunities for performance improvement breakthroughs. These potential interventions are aligned with the organization's strategic direction, goals, and values. Examples of these types of strategic interventions include the merging of cultures, improving employee and customer satisfaction, employee retention, and systems integration. The most senior consultants are needed to lead and support these large, complex initiatives. Relationship managers may participate in strategic performance improvement interventions or hand off the client to a consulting team. An RM can be selected to be involved in HPI interventions based on competencies and experience. Key clients with strategic business responsibilities are assigned the most seasoned RMs.

Tactically, the role of the RM is to continuously assess business needs, communicate those needs within the HPI department and serve as a broker of HPI talent on the client's behalf. One important responsibility is to assist the HPI department in providing clients with timely responsiveness and improved service quality. Periodic check-ins with the client on the quality of performance support received from the HPI department are important for problem resolution. At the end of an intervention, the RM debriefs the client and the consulting team on what went well, identifies recommended improvements, and communicates lessons learned.

Action Step 2: Identify Potential RMs

One of the most important selection decisions that an HPI leader makes is the assignment of RMs. They play a large part in creating a successful future for the new HPI department. The HPI leader assigns RMs to this role after a careful assessment of each consultant's

- ✦ competencies
- ✦ experience
- ✦ sales and service and rapport-building behaviors
- ✦ business knowledge and understanding of the organization's strategic direction, and business model and how key clients achieve their goals
- ✦ timely responsiveness
- ✦ ability to handle conflict and overcome client objections
- ✦ oral and written communication and strong analytical skills.

Part of the RM selection process is the ability of each candidate to self-assess strengths and weaknesses. Self-awareness is an important source of strength for the newly assigned RM. What are strengths and weaknesses in working with clients? What are negative self-programs or doubts on knowledge, skills, and abilities? Working with clients from the basis of maximizing strengths, and acknowledging and improving weaknesses sets the stage for strong client partnerships built on mutual respect and credibility.

Action Step 3: Prepare a Performance Model for the RMs

Often an HPI leader will develop an RM performance model. It is particularly useful in defining new, start-up positions. Normally an HPI leader creates a performance model by interviewing exemplary performers to determine what they do and how they do it. In most organizations with newly formed HPI departments, there are no exemplary RMs. Another approach is to interview exemplary RMs in other organizations. Although adjustments need to be made for differences in culture and business models, this is a rich source of data for the HPI leader. The HPI leader may also decide to find a position similar to the RM within the organization. Sales and service business units are a good source of exemplary performers with duties and performance expectations similar to the HPI department's RM.

The performance model outlines expected outcomes and critical duties, selection criteria, and success measures. It is used to create a competency-based job description and a selection profile listing education, experience required, and desired competencies. A performance scorecard of success measures for the position serves as a starting point for newly assigned RMs and their managers or coaches. As the cadre of RMs becomes more skilled and experienced, the performance model is updated.

Special preparation is sometimes required for those individuals assigned to a specialized consulting role such as RM. It is important for a new RM to understand what is different about the performance expectations of the new role. There are also new skills and success measures associated with being a RM. An RM workshop focusing on role clarity, critical skills to perform the role, and basic sales and service is an excellent investment in helping RMs effectively partner with clients (chapter 6).

Action Step 4: Build Components for the Partnering and Contracting Phase

The partnering and contracting phase of the HPI process guides the new consultant on reactive and proactive approaches to client relationships. Reactive approaches to the relationship probably already exist and may be the norm. Clients see that they need help and contact the HPI department to discuss performance problems. The proactive approach is used by consultants to seek out the client on performance gaps or as a routine method of assessing needs and communicating. Usually the consultant needs to be proactive in identifying potential performance gaps with the client. Being proactive as a performance consultant also means selling the new HPI process to clients at every opportunity. Effective consultants use both approaches—reactive and proactive—to support client business needs. Regardless of the approach, the quality and timeliness of the consultant's response must delight the client.

Initial and Continuing Client Meetings

This initial client meeting always requires a great deal of preparation. Relationship managers often use a checklist to walk through and plan each step before meeting with the client. Table 7-1 is a sample checklist of meeting preparation steps that are often considered by RMs. This checklist is used to prepare for any type of client meeting including an initial client meeting, a meeting to discuss specific performance gaps, or regular client update meetings. It is useful to walk through each step on the checklist, mark those steps that apply to the upcoming meeting, and script certain points for discussion.

Relationship managers conduct scripting sessions to determine the best possible approach for achieving their meeting goals with clients. Scripting involves creating an outline and highlighting talking points for the initial client meeting. Scripting statements explain to the client the role of an RM. The RM prepares questions to determine the client's needs and formulates steps and statements to obtain client agreement on next steps. This degree of preparation gives the RM the confidence to establish a strong first impression during the initial meeting. Often new RMs anticipate that clients harried by the demands of running a business will not devote the time needed for meetings. The RM can overcome this concern through diligent preparation and by appreciation of the value added by the client's time and effort.

The scripting session begins by dividing a group of RMs into triads. Each group works on the scripting exercises by listing content on index

100

Table 7-1. Relationship manager checklist for client meetings.

Step	Initial Meeting	Continuing Meetings
1. Identify key clients and build rapport	Yes	Yes
2. Explain and re-explain the RM's role	Yes	Yes
3. Focus on client business needs and ask the client what success looks like	Yes	Yes
4. Make contracting a natural part of the meeting	Yes	Yes
5. Write down key points and agreements	Yes	Yes
6. Conduct regular meetings on set days each month		Yes
7. Check in informally with the client		Yes
8. Move the client away from training as the only answer	Yes	Yes
9. Use the contract to keep agreed actions on track		Yes
10. Establish joint ownership for success		Yes

cards, sorting the cards, and clustering the responses. The large group reconvenes, and each triad briefs the group on scripted statements. The group selects the final scripted options, which are then summarized in a client meeting preparation document. This approach allows each RM to learn new partnering skills, continue to break down silos within the HPI department and with clients, and share knowledge from the different HPI functions.

When to Exit the Process

Are there situations where the RM should walk away from the client and exit the process? Absolutely! Not every request from a client for support is appropriate as a performance consulting intervention. Initial perceptions on a consulting opportunity by an RM do not always work out. How does the RM know when to pull the plug? What are the HPI department's policies and procedures for walking away from the client? How does the RM break the news to the client without damaging the relationship? These questions need to be answered in a consulting team meeting before giving the client bad news.

First, be sure that exiting the process is the right thing to do. It is best to let the client know that the HPI department cannot provide direct support if the RM encounters the following:

- ✦ The client does not have the authority to move forward. In other words, the RM is not dealing with the real client.
- ✦ The client refuses to jointly own with the HPI department the appropriate next step or action in the process.
- ✦ The client's issues or concerns are not performance-based, cannot be quantified, or the client does not want to measure the results.
- ✦ The scope or complexity of the intervention is beyond the technical capabilities of the HPI department.
- ✦ The HPI department and the client lack the resources to successfully complete the provisions of the contract.

If any of these situations exist, it is advisable for the RM to have a meeting with the client to discuss the appropriateness of a consulting intervention. Rehearse ahead of time exactly what needs to be said. In the meeting it is important to summarize briefly the steps leading up to the current status of work performed on the client's behalf. State the early assumptions that the RM and the client had in working together on the issues. Talk about the current status of the initiative, the findings, and your conclusion that moving forward is not advisable. Explain that the time, energy, resources, and morale of the client's team and the HPI department will be wasted on an intervention that yields disappointing results.

Depending on the client's level of insistence on continuing with the intervention and the risks of walking away, the performance consultant may decide with the client to provide limited assistance for a specific outcome. Carefully outline the expectations of the client on this limited project in the revised contract. If the HPI department's involvement still isn't feasible, it may be in everyone's best interest to transfer the client to an external partner. Once the client is effectively linked with the external partner, don't abandon the client! Be sure to periodically check in with the external partner and the client to ensure that the client is receiving appropriate support. Be there to continue giving the client advice while probing for additional needs. As the client's RM, reinforce through words and actions that although the HPI department could not support the client in this situation, the relationship with the client is valued.

The Contract

Assuming that none of these exit situations occur, proceed with the client in developing a performance improvement contract. A contract is used in each phase of the process to detail the agreements outlined in the client meeting. The contract from the initial client meeting becomes the blueprint for data collection and reporting in the assessment phase of the HPI process. The contract with the client defines roles, defines expectations and goals, establishes ground rules on measurement, and sets times for meetings and follow-up communication. The stronger the relationship between the RM and the client, the easier it is to reach agreement on a contract.

The contract should always include a cover memorandum to the client that summarizes the scope of work, comments on the relationship, and any special issues. A typical performance improvement contract contains the following provisions:

- ✦ purpose
- ✦ assumptions
- ✦ key actions and success measures
- ✦ timeline
- ✦ communication plan
- ✦ people resources (client, HPI consultants, internal partners, external partners)
- ✦ financial resources (project costs, source of funds, how much, identity of the signing/approving authority)
- ✦ equipment and facilities required
- ✦ next meeting (deliverables, participants, date/time, location).

Clients expect quick turnaround on results and sometimes have an attention span measured in minutes. To allow time for the consulting team to work through the HPI process properly, the performance consultant may decide during the contract discussions that the circumstances warrant offering the client some near-term solutions or quick hits. This may satisfy the client's desire for immediate action. If this step is taken, be sure that the near-term actions fit into the anticipated long-term actions that the consulting team is considering. This approach buys time to work with the client on longer-term actions that close performance gaps and provide sustainable results.

Action Step 5: Provide for RM Performance Feedback

The need for client feedback on the value and effectiveness of the RM role is essential for success in client partnering. The HPI leader and RMs often use a client satisfaction survey to obtain this feedback. The survey is sent via email to each client on a quarterly basis. Usually clients can complete the survey in 5 to 7 minutes. Figure 7-1 presents an example of a client satisfaction survey on the role and effectiveness of RMs.

What level of client participation should be expected? What kind of responses can be anticipated? How valuable will the data be in helping improve the quality of service provided by RMs to clients?

The answers to these questions depend on several factors. If the guidelines presented in this chapter are used to make the survey user-friendly, then client participation will increase. The client's responsiveness also correlates highly to their favorable and unfavorable perceptions on the value of the RM's role. It is not uncommon to experience up to an 80 percent client survey participation rate.

Initially client ratings may average between a 3.0 and 4.0 on a 5.0 scale for the items in questions 2 (figure 7-1). Responses below a 3.0 are obviously improvement opportunities. Client comments on the survey usually indicate that having one proactive RM meeting each month is about right. More frequent meetings are acceptable when requested by the client. Comments from questions 5, 6, and 7 often reflect the need for RMs to demonstrate stronger business knowledge or communication skills. Alternatively, the RM may need to help the client better understand the RM's role. Clients are often complimentary of the efforts made to respond quickly to their needs and of the extra effort made to resolve issues raised by the client. Relationship managers need to contact their clients and thank them for the feedback. Remember that the client expects to see improvement.

The HPI leader compiles the data from the client satisfaction survey with a summary of client responses. The summary is sent directly to RMs and their managers. They are requested to review the data, write down questions, and come to the next RM meeting prepared for discussion. The developmental purpose of the survey and the uses of the data by the RM for professional growth are strongly reinforced by the HPI leader.

The HPI leader provides a general overview of the summary data to all of the RMs at the next RM meeting. Client perceptions and trends are discussed. The HPI leader reinforces what is going well while spending most of the meeting on continuous improvement opportunities. Development opportunities are identified from this survey that cut across the RM team. These development needs are addressed in the RM workshop (chapter 6) and in a series of brown-bag meetings. Each RM is responsible for using the survey results for purposes of self-development. The HPI leader asks each manager and team leader to provide RMs with coaching and developmental support.

Figure 7-1. Example client satisfaction survey.

1. How well do you understand the role of your RM?

   _____ not at all   _____ somewhat   _____ fairly well   _____ well   _____ very well

2. Please rate the service provided by your RM in using the following scale:

   5 = far exceeds expectations
   4 = exceeds
   3 = achieves
   2 = marginally achieves
   1 = fails to achieve

   a) Proactively meeting with me at least once monthly _____
   b) Asking the right questions to assess my needs _____
   c) Demonstrating an understanding of my business needs _____
   d) Serving as a broker to obtain appropriate HPI support _____
   e) Ensuring that I received the agreed-upon HPI support _____
   f) Providing information routinely on HPI initiatives/capabilities _____
   g) Overall rating of RM service quality _____

3. How many times monthly does your RM meet with you? (please check ✓)

   Face-to-face meetings   _____1   _____2   _____3 or more   _____0
   Telephone or e-mail   _____1   _____2   _____3 or more   _____0

4. Is the frequency of contact between you and your RM . . .

   _____too frequent   _____just right   _____too infrequent   _____nonexistent?

5. What does your RM do that you believe is noteworthy?

6. What suggestions do you have to improve the quality of RM support?

7. Are you willing to take a few minutes quarterly to respond to this survey?

   _____yes   _____no   Client name: _____

Thank you for completing this survey. The results will be shared with the RM and used for developmental purposes.

Action Step 6: Apply Your Knowledge to a Case Study

 Relationship managers often find that much of their time is spent helping clients understand the business unit's performance gaps. Influencing the client to the possibility that a business or performance need exists and that something can be done about it is one of the early challenges faced by the RM. An example is the situation of Susan, a business division manager, facing poor results in revenue growth and profitability. Harry, Susan's new RM, overhears a conversation between two of Susan's direct reports commenting on the earnings pressure Susan faces. Harry looks into the performance data and finds that the division as a whole is under target by 8 percent for the first quarter and is continuing that trend through the middle of the second quarter. He quickly contacts several business colleagues in competing companies to benchmark the success of Susan's counterparts. He finds that their performance is on target and, in many cases, exceeding their organization's expectations.

Harry schedules his first monthly RM meeting with Susan. After building rapport, Harry clarifies his role as Susan's RM. He explains that in his previous role as an instructional designer, he provided skills and knowledge support for her employees. Now, as her RM, his role involves understanding her business needs and helping her leverage resources and support within the HPI department and the rest of the organization. Harry further explains that his job is to serve as a communication link between Susan and her division and the HPI department. This explanation of his new role is important for Harry in repositioning his value to Susan as a performance consultant. She needs to understand this new role and then see Harry deliver these new products and services in support of her business goals.

Harry changes the direction of the conversation. He casually mentions that during a review of the organization's first quarter data, he noticed that Susan's division was under its revenue target. Harry asks her about her business goals, performance-to-date against those goals, and her thoughts on performance issues. As Susan talks about her goals, Harry helps Susan position her business goals and results into performance language. He uses a relationship map that outlines the should/is performance gap. The map helps Harry with an approach to capturing Susan's operational goals and employee performance expectations so that she can see business improvement opportunities. Susan acknowledges that first quarter sales are usually sluggish and talks about the normal up-tick in momentum and earnings that usually occurs in subsequent quarters. Susan emphasizes her belief that most of the problem is with marketplace performance. She further states that her competitors are probably not doing any better.

Harry, with great tact, uses the preliminary data he collected to have Susan reflect on her business situation. After learning that her competitors appear to be making or exceeding their goals, Susan asks how this is possible. Harry explains that he isn't sure why there is a gap, but he would like to dig into it a little more and come back to her with thoughts on how they can work together to find out. Susan agrees and they schedule a follow-up meeting.

Harry has proactively identified a critical performance gap and impressed Susan by his approach, preparation, and interest. She agrees to an initial consulting meeting. The purpose of this meeting is to clarify performance issues, reach an agreement on next steps to be taken to gather data on the performance problem, and determine role clarity among Harry, the HPI department, Susan, and her direct reports.

To prepare for the initial meeting, Harry scripts his transition statement reaffirming his role as Susan's RM and clarifying the value that the HPI department can bring to supporting her business unit's performance gaps. He carefully outlines questions to supplement his knowledge of Susan's key goals, her issues, and her level of understanding on general causes of the gap. Harry writes out his main points on the benchmarking he has done and some of the implications for Susan's business unit. He drafts bullet points on a contract to collect additional data on causes of the performance gap. Harry prepares a more complete relationship map that outlines his understanding of the should/is gap for Susan's performance problems. He will use the map during the meeting to get Susan's help in capturing her operational goals, employee performance expectations, and the current gaps in both sets of goals. This technique should help Susan to identify business improvement opportunities.

Harry's final preparation involves a walkthrough rehearsal and critique with another performance consultant. He repeats this walkthrough separately with a line manager. This is a critical step for Harry to ensure that he has covered all of the bases from a business perspective. Now he believes that he is ready for the initial consulting meeting with Susan. Harry's plan for the initial meeting is to present Susan with enough preliminary data on potential internal performance gaps and competitor performance data that she will contract with Harry on doing a performance improvement intervention.

The contract will focus on doing the next step in the HPI process—collecting and gathering data—to assess the root causes of performance gaps.

Progress Milestones

In this chapter you learned that establishing and maintaining strong client partnerships is a fundamental prerequisite for successfully implementing HPI interventions. The trust and credibility between RM and client makes all the difference in the RM's ability to successfully meet or exceed the client's expectations of the HPI department. The very act of partnering with clients, the preparation and development of scripts, and the development of sales and service skills draws practitioners and functions out of silos into working as part of one integrated HPI team.

Effective partnerships are based on your identification of client needs and performance gaps, and determining the root causes of those gaps. Chapter 8 will outline process steps for your review in root-cause identification, assessment, and analysis. You probably already know the value of conducting a needs assessment. For the HPI department, root-cause assessment is a value-added component of the performance improvement process that moves the client away from preconceived notions about a solution to a data-based assessment of the causes and appropriate actions for complete performance support.

Key Points of This Chapter

✔ Select and assign consultants representing all areas of the HPI department, who are knowledgeable on the new HPI process and possess strong analytical, sales, and service skills, to key clients. Establish and maintain long-term strategic partnerships for the future success of the HPI department.

✔ Build a performance model to serve as a guide for the selection, development, and role clarity of RMs.

✔ Invest in the long-term competency development of the RMs. Build formal and on-the-job learning and development opportunities to create and sustain effective relationships.

✔ Relationship managers and other performance consultants must continuously share lessons learned in establishing and maintaining strong business partnerships.

✔ Communicate the purpose, benefits, and early successes of RMs throughout the organization and within the HPI department.

✔ Reward and recognize RM results based on measures of client satisfaction.

8

Gathering and Assessing Data: Separating Fact From Fiction

In chapter 7 you learned how to develop partnerships with key clients, the importance of educating clients on multiple causes of performance gaps, and the need to use the HPI process to investigate root causes in a systematic way. So after spending all that time educating clients on the HPI process, why do some clients continue to approach you with a performance problem and offer the solution in the same breath? Clients often appear conditioned to invest people, money, and time for a single-event solution, such as training, in the hope that it will cure their performance problems. In many organizations, HPI practitioners, particularly trainers, often willingly oblige. After all, if training will make the client happy and we are able to do it, then why not? Sometimes there is a short-term lift in performance. Unfortunately, in a few months many of these clients are back looking for another expensive "fix."

What's wrong with this picture? Why do we as performance consultants allow this scenario to occur year after year within our organizations? What can performance consultants do to change current performance support practices so that there is a different future for the HPI department? How can we teach clients that multiple actions are usually required to improve performance? What can be done to convince the client that when training is part of the solution, changes in the work environment are required for sustainable results?

The answers to these questions lie in your learning and applying a systematic approach to gathering and assessing data. This systematic approach helps the client identify root causes and take appropriate actions to close performance gaps. It is indispensable to the client's success. The strength of your client relationship allows you to influence the client to use the assessment tools and methods of the new HPI process for designing complete performance solutions. Collecting and analyzing data objectively separates fact from fiction. It moves the client away from preconceived notions on the type of performance support needed. In this chapter you will have the opportunity to reflect on approaches to gathering and assessing data, as well as implementing cause analysis that you can introduce to your organization.

 ## Action Steps to Gathering and Assessing Data

1. Form the data collection team.
2. Build and implement the data collection plan.
3. Review the data with the client.
4. Contract with the client for implementing an HPI intervention.
5. Apply your knowledge to a case study.

The steps in the data collection phase of the HPI process provide you with the tools needed to gather the facts on your client's performance problems. This phase of the process establishes a partnership with the client on ownership of the methodology and data on root causes to identify actions needed to improve business unit results.

Action Step 1: Form the Data Collection Team

The HPI leader is responsible for selecting the data collection team leader. Often the HPI leader will recommend two team co-leaders to the client. A senior performance consultant from the HPI department serves as one co-leader, and a senior manager from the client's business unit serves as the other. The line co-leader is the expert in business unit processes, is credible within the organization, and has a reputation for objectivity. The HPI co-leader is an experienced performance consultant with strong competencies in the development and implementation of data collection plans. Both leaders are capable project managers with analytical and coaching skills.

For the client and the HPI leader it is advantageous to have a line co-leader on the data collection team. From the HPI leader's standpoint, the line co-leader helps the team gain acceptance within the business unit and lessens resistance to data collection. Doors are opened for identifying and scheduling the right audience to participate in data collection activities. Ownership in fulfilling the contract is vested in both the business unit and the HPI department. From the client's perspective the line co-leader decreases his/her anxiety on lack of control in data gathering within the business unit. Client concerns about the objectivity of data collection methods and the sorting and analysis of the data are minimized with a trusted line manager involved in the process. The client is reassured that the business view is well represented in all aspects of the data collection team's activities.

Table 8-1 lists some of the roles that may be assigned to the data collection consulting team. This information is presented as an example of the talent that is needed to implement a successful data collection plan.

The data collection team leader may select performance consultants to serve on the team in the roles of process facilitator, interviewer, data analyst, and evaluator. The composition of the team depends on the data collection plan and methods specified in the contract. It is important to include practitioners with competencies in TQM, OD, ISD, industrial psychology, and knowledge management on the data collection team. They contribute diverse expertise in data collection sources, methods, research techniques, needs assessment, design of survey instruments, cause analysis, group facilitation, and statistical analysis. Creating the data collection team is another of those critical integration opportunities that breaks down functional silos.

Action Step 2: Build and Implement the Data Collection Plan

The data collection team develops a plan of action to ensure that the right data is collected and that it is collected properly in accordance with the client contract. The plan is the data collection team's blueprint for meeting the client's expectations of timely, objective, and actionable data. It is developed with the active involvement of the consultants on the team. It is essential to the success of the team that the client's input is requested. The

Table 8-1. Data collection consulting team roles.

Role	Duty
Team Leader	Responsible for developing the data collection plan that supports the client contract. Includes managing the plan, making team member assignments, coaching, coordinating, and managing resources
Interviewer	Demonstrates expertise in data collection sources and methods, questioning techniques, and meeting facilitation
Analyst	Determines data collection sources and methods, conducts data sorting exercises, analyzes data, and summarizes findings
Designer	Conducts audience analysis and designs survey instruments, focus group sessions, questions, and exercises
Process Facilitator	Provides expertise in focus group and meeting facilitation processes with clients, the consulting team, and performers

client also approves the plan before it is implemented. The plan becomes an operating matrix that is distributed to all team members and updated at data collection team meetings. Generally, a data collection plan consists of the following steps:

+ The team obtains industry research data and benchmarks peer organizations to determine issues relating to the client's potential performance gaps.
+ The team leader meets with the client to complete a relationship map. The map outlines the client's business unit should/is performance data.
+ From preliminary data gathered external to the organization and knowledge of business unit issues, the team's consultants identify general categories of data needed to identify internal and external root causes of performance gaps.
+ The team identifies the audience, sources, and methods of data collection and establishes a timeline and team accountabilities. The team also determines what resources—money, people, and equipment—will be needed for the data collection effort.
+ The team builds and tests appropriate data collection instruments and decides how to use these instruments with performers.
+ The team finalizes the data collection plan, which is then approved by the client.

Determine Performance and Process Gaps

The consulting team and client need to map out what is known about the client's goals, performance expectations, and current level of performance. This helps identify which data is needed to determine root causes of performance gaps. The consultant and the client identify the operational goals of the organization, goals of the client's business unit, and performer expectations. These operational goals are stated as business needs and the performer goals as performance needs. These goals represent the future or desired state, the "should" performance on a relationship map. The results achieved to date become the "is," or the current performance data. The difference or gap between the "should" and the "is" becomes the target of opportunity for the client and the data collection team.

Determine Causes

What are the sources of data available for determining the causes of performance gaps? What are the data collection methods used to gather the right data for the client's specific performance problems? Table 8-2 contains an example of some of the data sources available for consultant use. It is the team leader's responsibility to use the rich diversity of data collection sources provided by the HPI practitioners assigned to the team.

Experienced consultants gather external data early in the process to avoid duplicating data that is expensive and time-consuming to collect. Benchmarking data is collected through a variety of external agencies, peer organizations, and professional associations. External agencies include local, state, and government agencies, for-profit research companies, and professional associations (appendix C). Professional associations, such as ASTD, ISPI, and the Society for Human Resources Management (SHRM), have developed excellent research capabilities and sources of information. Customized research may be requested through these and other professional associations that directly support HPI interventions. Other sources of data include networking through peers at competitor organizations and at companies with the reputation for conducting internal performance consulting. Performance consulting initiatives on organization-wide performance problems are remarkably similar regardless of industry. The data collected on a performance gap at one organization often has application to similar performance gaps being analyzed by the HPI data collection team.

It is unlikely that performance consultants will find all the data they need for supporting a consulting intervention from external sources. Skills

Table 8-2. Data sources for the should/is performance analysis.

Source Category	Data Source
Performers Exceeding Expectations	• exemplary performers • managers of exemplary performers • direct reports of exemplary performers • peers of exemplary performers
Performers Achieving Expectations	• typical performers • managers of typical performers • direct reports of typical performers • peers of typical performers
Clients	• internal to organization • external to organization
Subject Matter Experts	• internal to organization • external to organization
Benchmarking	• between internal business units • external—peer organizations, associations, universities, best in class industry leaders

and knowledge in the collection and analysis of internal sources of data are essential to the success of the data collection team. Experienced consultants often select a minimum of two data collection methods for each performance gap. They use exemplary performers whenever possible as a vital source of valuable data. Exemplary performers are individuals who exceed expectations as measured against department goals. They have figured out how to exceed expectations in a department where barriers to performance prevent typical performers from accomplishing their goals. Comparing exemplary and typical performer data is essential to the team's success in determining the root causes of the should/is performance gap.

Consultants on the data collection team need to be comfortable in the design and development of a wide variety of methods and tools for supporting the client's assessment requirements. Table 8-3 lists a sample of data collection methods and tools that are often available to performance consultants. Consultants from the HPI functions work together to create a rich menu of tools and assessment capabilities.

Action Step 3: Review the Data With the Client

The team meets to analyze and sort the data. Team members with a quality and marketing research background are particularly skilled at using analytical tools to bring clarity to masses of raw data. Eliminate data that is not actionable or is superfluous to the client's performance problems. Put the data on index cards, affix the cards to the wall, and then sort the data by broad themes. The consulting team can brainstorm each category of data to ensure that all patterns in the data are identified. Summarize the data and prepare a report for your client's data-reporting meeting.

Table 8-3. Data collection methods and tools.

Method	Tools
Internal (On the Job)	<ul><li>observation checklist</li><li>one-on-one interviews</li><li>focus groups</li><li>questionnaires/surveys</li><li>quality tools, including praedo charts, scatter diagrams, affinity diagrams, histograms, and brainstorming</li></ul>
External	<ul><li>review of the literature (books and journals)</li><li>Internet</li></ul>
Industry Data	<ul><li>for-profit research</li><li>shared industry reports and studies</li></ul>

The data collection team leader should prepare an agenda outlining the key steps in the data-reporting meeting. Table 8-4 lists critical steps that are often included in the data-reporting agenda. The team meets to script and rehearse the meeting. Think like the client and view the patterns of the data from the client's perspective. Spend the time necessary to truly understand the data and its implications for the client's performance problems. Carefully prepare the script so that bias is eliminated in reporting the results. In addition to the team leader, determine who will co-facilitate the meeting with the client.

The facilitators should rehearse each step of the data-reporting meeting. The success of the meeting depends on detailed preparation and objectivity in presenting the data. The price of poor preparation is a level of anxiety and lack of facilitator confidence that could lead to a disastrous client meeting.

Action Step 4: Contract With the Client on the Intervention

The primary outcome for the data-reporting meeting is a contract with the client to implement actions based on the data. But what happens if the client chokes? What does the consultant do if the client signals that he or she isn't ready to move forward? The performance consultant must persevere in those

Table 8-4. The data-reporting meeting agenda.

Agenda Item	Topics
Purpose of the Meeting	• anticipated outcomes • scope of the intervention
Methodology	• audience and sources of data • data collection methods
Summary of the Findings	• a brief statement of the themes and major findings • enhancers and barriers to performance
Detailed Findings	• verbatim quotes • data segmented by audience and source
Interpretation of the Data	• data presented with objectivity • client perspective • consultant perspective
Conclusions	• actions • priorities • contract on intervention actions • next steps

instances where the client may hesitate to act even when the data is compelling and needed actions appear clear. With belief in the validity of the data collection and assessment process and relying on the original contract, provide the performance consultant with the framework for negotiating with the client on actions to improve performance. The case study presents an example of how a data collection team dealt with this type of situation.

Action Step 5: Apply Your Knowledge to a Case Study

 Harry is Susan's relationship manager. Susan is the senior manager of a business unit and a critical client. Their experience serves as an example of how data collection techniques were applied to a problem of employee retention. Prior to his current job as an instructional designer and role as relationship manager, Harry was a business analyst. His instructional design skills, analyst experience, and growing knowledge of the business make him a valuable resource for the data collection team. So instead of handing off the client after completing the data collection contract as relationship managers sometimes do, Harry is asked by Linda, the HPI leader, to become the data collection team leader. Harry agrees and begins to select team members and build a data collection plan.

Harry and the team's consultants agree that the data needed to support Susan can best be collected through focus groups. Conducting focus groups is a valuable tool for collecting data. A focus group is a facilitated meeting of performers for the purpose of identifying root causes and recommending actions to close performance gaps. The team designs the sessions around three focus groups. The focus groups include exemplary performers, typical performers currently employed, and performers who left the organization within the past six months.

Harry selects two consultants from the team to facilitate the focus groups. Facilitator preparation includes meeting logistics planning, participant selection, facilitation skills, and the communication plan. The facilitators, with Harry's help, prepare the agenda and create a script. The script is designed to elicit the information necessary to analyze the root causes for the turnover problem (table 8-5).

The facilitators conduct a final rehearsal of the script in a meeting attended by the data collection team. The team provides a critique as the last quality check used by the facilitators to ensure that all steps and standards in the process are followed correctly.

Table 8-5. The focus group session script.

Agenda Item	Talking Points
Welcome	• Introduce process facilitators • What are we here to accomplish?
Objectives	• Participants can have complete confidence in the objectivity and privacy of the process. • Identify what the organization is doing and not doing to retain employees. • Identify and prioritize recommendations for what the organization should do to retain employees and improve their performance.
Background	• The organization has been through numerous changes over the past couple of years. • One of the consequences of this change is the effect on employee retention. The organization wants to do a better job of keeping our employees. • We what to know the barriers existing within the company to long-term employee retention. • We are very interested in your objective recommendations on what should be done by the organization to improve.
Participant Benefits	• You are here representing every employee in the organization. • This is your opportunity to have a positive effect on changing your own work environments and on the success of the organization.
Ground Rules	• All the information we discuss is recorded in general terms and then is pooled and used to produce a report. • Don't use individual names. Confidentiality is protected at all times. • Everyone participates. • Be completely objective and open with your feedback.
Survey Instrument (See Figure 8.1.)	The facilitator introduces the survey instrument, asks the participants to read through each item, and answers any participant questions. Each individual completes the survey and then the results are put on a chart by the facilitator to stimulate discussion.
Interactive Session (with one facilitator asking questions of the group and the second facilitator serving as recorder)	• Of all the places you could have worked, why did you decide to come to work at this organization? • What is the organization doing that motivates you want to continue working here? • What is the organization doing that is a barrier to your retention? • What are the "Big Five" actions that should be taken now to address the most important problem areas? • What other recommendations do you have to improve employee satisfaction and retention?
Facilitated Discussion	• Chart participant responses to each question, discuss, and prioritize for action.
Closing Statement	• Next step for the team is to prepare a summary report. • The report will be presented to senior management. • The team appreciates your participation, your time, and feedback.

Figure 8-1. The focus group survey instrument.

Please give us feedback on your satisfaction with the work environment factors you encounter on the job. Rate your job position by rank-ordering each of the 10 areas of the work environment as they affect employee retention.

Rank Order (1–10)	Work Environment Factors	Satisfaction Level Unsatisfied Satisfied (circle your answer)				
	Received appropriate leader support and coaching	1	2	3	4	5
	Feel your work is appreciated by your immediate supervisor	1	2	3	4	5
	You know how to identify opportunities for advancement	1	2	3	4	5
	You are encouraged to take advantage of opportunities for advancement	1	2	3	4	5
	Received training and development appropriate to achieve expectations	1	2	3	4	5
	Employee benefits appropriate to you and your family's needs	1	2	3	4	5
	Performance of other employees met your expectations	1	2	3	4	5
	Performance of your managers met your expectations	1	2	3	4	5
	Base pay is appropriate for duties and performance expected	1	2	3	4	5
	Incentive program is appropriate for your contribution to the organization	1	2	3	4	5

Armed with the data from the focus group, Harry, as the team leader, prepares an executive summary of the team's findings to present to Susan. Harry also serves as the lead facilitator of the data reporting meeting. He covers the points outlined in the script and moves through each step of the agenda listed in table 8-4. The presentation is more of an open discussion with frequent questions from Susan and her direct reports.

Harry presents an executive summary of the findings. There are five issues that contribute to employee turnover in Susan's business unit. These issues are stress in the workplace, low staffing, pay, the sales culture, and poor leadership. Detailed data is attached to the executive summary. Harry uses the detailed information to help Susan interpret the data and to respond to clarifying questions.

Susan compliments Harry on the data collection team's results. She is pleased with the quality of the data and his style of presentation.

She agrees with the sources and methods used to collect the data. Susan also reaffirms that the level of turnover is unacceptably high. The causes of turnover and actions to address the root causes are now quite clear to Susan and to her managers.

Harry moves the conversation to the contract on intervention actions and is surprised when Susan, his client, hesitates. Susan believes that there are at present too many competing demands for resources to be devoted to action planning on turnover. She tells Harry that she wants to wait. In 6 months or so, the timing may be better to implement his recommendations. Susan indicates that there are some training actions in progress, such as a new leadership development program, that bring enough change to begin decreasing turnover.

Harry is surprised and momentarily at a loss. The data is compelling, the client has agreed with the methodology, the quality of the data, and the implications. What is going on here? He decides to push back. The best he is able to do is to get Susan to agree to another meeting in 2 weeks. They agree that the agenda for this meeting is to review the progress of current actions in place and again discuss the possibility of contracting for new actions to reduce turnover.

What are Harry's options? He can exit the process because it appears the client does not want to own the results and take appropriate action. In reviewing all of the work done by the team, the quality of the data, the conclusions generated, and the organizational business need to reduce turnover and improve sales results, Harry is reluctant to walk away. He decides to keep this option open. If he cannot convince Susan at the next meeting to be a stakeholder in contracting for improvement actions, then the consulting team will move on to other initiatives.

The consulting team meets to list assumptions and possible courses of action. They decide that Susan may be afraid of failure and that many of the actions based on the data will require her and her key managers to change their style of leadership and make substantial changes in the work environment. Harry contacts Susan and discusses meeting one-on-one with her direct reports to prepare for the next meeting. She concurs, and Harry meets with each of Susan's direct reports. They review the data and the actions needed to counteract root causes and build a tentative approach to implementing these changes. The majority of Susan's direct reports agree to support developing a contract on these actions.

At the follow-up meeting with Susan and her managers, Harry summarizes their main findings from the data, reviews the actions that appear consistent with that data, and presents a draft implementation contract. With the support of Susan's managers and Harry's assurance that the HPI department will partner with Susan through the end of the intervention, Susan agrees to move forward with the contract.

Progress Milestones

This chapter presents the argument that the integrity of the data collection team's efforts in determining the root causes of client performance gaps is essential to the success of the HPI department. The data collection and cause analysis you conduct for your clients is one of the great benefits provided by performance consultants. Clients often initially resist the time and expense associated with data collection. Sometimes, as was demonstrated in the case study with Susan, you must be tough, persistent, and act in accordance with the belief that you are in the right. In these moments of truth it is only through the strength of your relationship with the client that fear of the unknown or reluctance to change is overcome. With this approach your client has the information to make informed decisions on actions that are appropriate for improving employee performance and business results.

By partnering, contracting with the client, and gathering and assessing data, you establish the foundation for the implementation of intervention actions to improve performance. Chapter 9 examines the various intervention actions needed for complete solutions to your client's performance problems. This sets the stage for the design, development, and delivery of these actions by a performance consulting team and client to improve results.

Key Points of This Chapter

✔ Partner with a client who has a performance problem that is manageable, within the assessment competencies and capabilities of the HPI team, and with a client willing to commit the resources necessary for collecting and analyzing root-cause data.

✔ Build an HPI assessment cross-functional team representative of the diverse competencies and tools of the performance improvement functions and internal partners in the organization.

✔ Invest in the competencies of the more experienced practitioners so they can serve as data collection and analysis mentors for others on the data collection team.

✔ Anticipate and deal with client resistance on the time and expense associated with collecting data.

✔ Continuously educate and sell the client on the data collection and assessment methods of the HPI process.

✔ Ensure that the data collection team works closely with the client in developing a data collection plan.

✔ Build data collection templates to streamline the data collection process. Use quality tools in collecting, sorting, and analyzing data.

✔ Prepare an executive summary of key points with detailed data attached to help the client see patterns in the data.

✔ Before conducting the data collection analysis meeting with the client, rehearse, and rehearse, and rehearse. Use the client's time well.

✔ Always present the facts without bias. Allow the client to reach conclusions objectively.

✔ Be sure the client takes ownership of the data and its implications.

✔ End the data-reporting meeting with a draft contract that outlines implementation actions based on the data.

9

Implementing HPI Interventions

This is the point in the HPI process that you have worked so hard to reach. The client is ready to move forward with you in implementing a performance improvement intervention. You have established a partnership with your client and collected, analyzed, and reported the data successfully. The client understands the implications of the data. The client agrees with you about the need to identify and implement actions to close performance gaps. How do you as the consulting team leader or as a performance consultant move the process forward to implement intervention actions with clients that improve performance? This chapter provides an approach for you and your clients to consider as you build and implement performance improvement interventions.

Action Steps for Implementing the Unified HPI Approach

1. Select the best practitioners to form the first consulting team and work with the client on understanding the HPI process.
2. Build an implementation plan for a performance improvement intervention.
3. Develop intervention actions to improve performance.
4. Apply your knowledge to a case study.

Action Step 1: Form the Consulting Implementation Team

Building an implementation team and plan are essential first steps for the consulting team leader. A unique set of competencies and experiences is required for consulting team members to build intervention actions that will have a bottom-line effect on business. Consultants must be carefully selected for competencies that cut across the process, performance, and skills-and-knowledge actions of the HPI process. This cross-section of competencies and experience requires a team of consultants representing all of the HPI functions, the client's business unit, HPI network partners, and external alliance partners.

The team leader organizes the diverse roles and competencies represented on the consulting team for maximum effectiveness. The implementation consulting team (table 9-1) is often structured into three groups depending on the size and complexity of the intervention.

Leadership Group

A leadership group comprising the team leader and sub-team leaders is responsible for fulfilling the specifications of the client contract and developing and successfully implementing the intervention plan. The senior sub-team leader stands ready to serve as a substitute for the team leader or replace the team leader if required. Administrative and technical specialists are attached to the leadership group for guidance and assignments.

TEAM LEADER. The HPI leader selects the consulting team leader. The implementation phase of the HPI process requires a team leader with strong leadership, consulting, and interpersonal skills. The team leader recruits, selects, develops, and coaches team members. The team leader assigns roles to sub-team leaders and to team members. The leader sets goals, coaches the sub-

Table 9-1. Intervention consulting team.

Leadership Group:	Staff:
Team leader Sub-team leaders	Evaluator Communications specialist Administrative specialist HPI network internal partners External alliance partners

Consulting Sub-Teams		
Skills and Knowledge	**Process**	**Performance**
Sub-team leader Instructional designer Performance technologist Facilitator/trainer Knowledge specialist Subject matter experts	Sub-team leader Information technology Process consultant (OD, TQM, engineering) Industrial psychologist Exemplary performers	Sub-team leader Performance consultants Strategic planner HR specialist

team leaders, and ensures that they coach their consultants. The team leader is ultimately responsible for the alignment of team activities and results with the strategic direction of the organization, the client's business model, and HPI department goals.

In addition to being the first among equals as the leader of the team, he or she is a project manager. Balancing the resources in people, time, budget, equipment, and facilities is required to effectively implement HPI interventions. A planning matrix with milestones is created as a project management tool. Sub-team leaders are assigned a series of actions, goals, deadlines, and resources as part of the implementation plan. The leadership group approves and implements a communication plan to keep team members, clients, the HPI department, and organization up-to-date on the progress of the intervention. The team and the sub-teams meet frequently to review issues, assignments, and determine progress.

SUB-TEAM LEADERS. Consultants serve as sub-team leaders because they demonstrate proficiency in the core HPI competencies and consulting tools required for the team's success. Sub-team leaders do not need to be former or current HPI managers. The team leader selects sub-team leaders based on their leadership, consulting, and project management credibility within the HPI department. This is a developmental opportunity for performance consultants who have the potential to become future HPI team leaders or department managers. Selecting sub-team leaders with performance improvement backgrounds from the HPI functions is another opportunity to break down silos and share diverse competencies and consulting tools. This is an integration opportunity that the HPI leader and team leaders must not squander.

SPECIALISTS. A small cadre of staff specialists works directly with the leadership group. The evaluator, communications specialist, and administrative specialist possess skills needed by the entire team. Line professionals from the client's business unit provide business competencies needed by the team. The HPI network service partners and external alliance partners provide resources and in-depth technical expertise (chapter 4).

The evaluator is the team's expert on the HPI scorecard. Evaluators are responsible for assisting consultants in developing scorecard tools for each intervention action. They support sub-team leaders and consultants in aligning intervention actions with the measurement plan. Evaluators directly perform and track measurement tasks for the team and report progress to the team leader. They assist the team and sub-team leaders in coaching the performance consultants and the client on the appropriate use of scorecard tools and techniques. Evaluators develop the measurement report based on scorecard results. They help the team leader talk the client through the measurement results and answer questions at the end of an intervention meeting.

One role on the consulting team often overlooked by the team leader is the communication specialist. The communicator for the team is often an internal network partner from the public relations or marketing departments. The communications specialist is responsible for developing the team's communication plan. The communication plan is the tool used by the team leader to keep the client, team members, and the HPI department up-to-date on progress, issues, and best practices. Communication promotes the benefits of the intervention and its implications for the organization and key clients. The communication specialist provides the team leader with valuable expertise for preparing for client update meetings, writing the contract document with clarity, and developing summaries of discussions and agreements from team meetings.

The prudent team leader provides for dedicated administrative support to the consulting team. In addition to handling the logistics of scheduling, facilities, equipment, and correspondence, the administrative specialist maintains and updates the implementation planning matrix. It is the administrative specialist's job to support each of the sub-teams. The more the team leader can relieve performance consultants of administrative tasks, the better he or she can concentrate on implementing and measuring performance improvement actions on behalf of clients.

The Sub-Teams

Consultants with expertise in each area of HPI may be divided into sub-teams to promote efficiency and effectiveness. The skills and knowledge improvement sub-team creates and implements learning and knowledge-based solutions. The process improvement sub-team focuses on systemic, procedural, and work-flow solutions. The performance improvement sub-team emphasizes solutions requiring change in client and leadership behaviors, HR actions, or change in the work environment. All three sub-teams integrate their actions so that the solutions being created maximize the bottom-line effect on the client's business results.

The skills and knowledge improvement team (table 9-2) provides solutions for performance problems caused by gaps in performer skills and knowledge. The solutions usually involve training design and delivery with a focus on specific skills or accessibility to facts and data that becomes part of the performer's required knowledge base. Sub-team members are often divided into content-specific and design-specific roles. The team members in the content-specific roles are knowledge management specialists and subject matter experts. These team members ensure that the content and knowledge designed and delivered to practitioners are appropriate for the performance expectations of the position. The design-specific roles of instructional designer, performance technologist, and facilitator/trainer focus on the skills needed by performers to achieve or exceed expectations. These team members design, develop, and deliver instructional products and programs that integrate with content-specific information.

Process improvement actions (table 9-3) are indispensable to the success of the intervention. It is rare that changes to organizational processes are not part of a comprehensive HPI intervention. Performance consultants on the process improvement sub-team usually have backgrounds in OD, TQM, systems engineering, or IT. They take a systematic view of process actions that leads to changes in workplace systems. These consultants develop and implement actions that provide for continuous improvement.

It is the team leader's responsibility to integrate the actions of the skills and knowledge and process improvement sub-teams with that of the performance improvement sub-team (table 9-4). As the integration of actions occurs, consultants and clients often note that the greatest effect on client goals is in process and performance improvement actions. This is because the work environment must change for complete, sustainable performance solutions to performance gaps. The development of skills-and-knowledge actions is closely coordinated so that only those actions necessary to support

Table 9-2. Skills and knowledge improvement sub-team roles.

Role	Responsibility
Instructional Designer	Designs and develops learning-based programs and performance support tools such as job aids, templates, and checklists
Performance Technologist	Designs and develops learning-based programs using e-learning delivery methods such as Web-based programs, CBT, electronic performance support, and intranet solutions
Facilitator/Trainer	Delivers instructional programs or facilitates skill-based sessions
Knowledge Management Specialist	Creates databases for the sharing of best practices, storage, retrieval, and analysis of information through various media including Web and intranet technology, job aids, and existing communication methods
Subject Matter Experts	Possess the technical expertise as a member of the client's department or as an external partner required to certify tasks, content, and procedures necessary for performance support

Table 9-3. Process improvement sub-team roles.

Role	Responsibility
Information Technology Specialist	Ensures that usability testing is conducted in reengineering the system to the performance needs of typical performers and provides technology delivery support
Process Consultant	Provides expertise in the redesign of work flow, systems, policies, and procedures, tasks and steps, and process facilitation to eliminate barriers to performance
Industrial Psychologist	Creates employee selection and testing processes that are aligned with the culture and work environment of the business unit; they provide support to the evaluator in creating measurement instruments and procedures for the HPI scorecard
Exemplary Performers	Individuals who consistently exceed expectations and contribute innovative solutions to performance barriers in the work environment

process and performance improvement changes are implemented. This eliminates costly development and delivery of training that often becomes a single-event solution yielding few long-term results. Integrating these actions is essential for delivering complete performance solutions to the client.

Action Step 2: Build an Implementation Plan

The consulting team leader, aided by the team's performance consultants, is responsible for developing a detailed implementation plan. Why take the time to do an implementation plan? It may seem unnecessary because important actions have already been identified in the contract. In balancing all that needs to be done along with the client's sense of urgency, the team leader often finds that just moving ahead aggressively feels like the right thing to do. It is easy to fall into this trap, but the price of not creating and executing an implementation plan is potentially very high. Without a detailed plan, the consulting team lacks focus and individual accountability for success. Clients become concerned when they observe inefficient, ineffective approaches to interventions of great importance to their business goals. All of the work previously completed is at risk without quality execution.

The implementation plan is the consulting team leader's blueprint for developing and doing intervention actions. Whether the team leader uses planning software or a stubby pencil, basic information is required to start

Table 9-4. Performance improvement sub-team roles.

Role	Responsibility
Performance Consultant	Builds competency and performance models to close performance gaps, validate performance expectations, and support revised selection, reward and recognition, performance management, and employee development models, and provides recommendations for changes to the work environment for sustainable results
Strategic Planner	Develops actions for closing organizational gaps in business unit plans and models that link business unit performance with the strategic direction of the organization
HR Specialist	Provides support for actions dealing with recruiting and retention, leadership development, reward and recognition, and performance management
Exemplary Performer	Individuals who have identified approaches to exceeding expectations by overcoming work environment barriers and maximizing work environment enhancers

the planning process. The core of the implementation plan stems from the client contract developed at the end of the data-reporting meeting. The team leader extracts the agreed-upon roles, responsibilities, tasks, and success measures from the contract. The team and sub-team leaders create a high-level set of milestones and a timeline for the team and each sub-team. The implementation plan should include the following:

+ What actions must the team take to meet or exceed client expectations outlined in the intervention contract?
+ What are the priorities of the consulting team?
+ What are the key accountabilities and priorities of each team member?
+ What does success look like for the client, the team, and the performance consultants? What is the HPI scorecard for the intervention?
+ What needs to be communicated and to whom? How frequently? What distribution channels are needed to reach the audience?
+ What resources, money, time, equipment, and facilities are needed for each intervention action? What is available? How do you bridge any gaps?
+ How often are team meetings scheduled and who must attend?

Team meetings are scheduled to build a detailed plan. Each sub-team meets to identify from the client contract the actions they are accountable for. Tasks and assignments are identified and prioritized. Each set of actions links to a menu of tools. The team may create new tools or customize existing tools to support the performance needs of the client. The team leader meets with the client to review and discuss the plan. Final client agreement on the plan is needed to start the intervention phase of the HPI process.

Action Step 3: Develop Intervention Actions

Table 9-5 contains a list of actions that may be used by performance consultants in HPI interventions. This table is not an exhaustive study of process improvement actions; rather, it is a generic list that the consulting team can customize to the client's needs. It presents examples of the types of actions that performance consultants have available in an integrated HPI process and HPI department. Not all of these actions apply to every intervention. These intervention actions become enhancers to employee performance by blending them into a complete solution to the client's performance problems.

Table 9-5. Actions to Improve Performance

Process Improvement	Performance Improvement	Skills and Knowledge Improvement
• goal setting and continuous improvement • policies and procedures • position workload, tasks, and accountabilities • staffing models and levels • systems and technology reengineering • workflow streamlining	**Client** • leadership actions: coaching, communication, team building • ownership of performance problems, solutions, and results • provision of resources: tools, equipment, facilities, and personnel for HPI interventions • leadership development **Human Resources** • performance management, reward and recognition system • employee selection model • employee retention model **Work environment** • competency and performance models • removal of employee stressors in the workplace • climate, ergonomics • scorecard of measures	• training curricula • workplace development • tools, job aids, and templates • knowledge management data • e-learning solutions including CBT, electronic performance support, Web-based and intranet learning

Process Improvement Actions

Consultants with formal preparation and experience in OD, industrial psychology, TQM, and IT provide the team with a systematic approach to analyzing and improving organizational and performer results in the workplace (table 9-6). They carefully study the documentation on policies, procedures, and workplace standards to determine how up-to-date, efficient, and effective these documents are as performance support tools. Usability testing is performed on critical technical systems to evaluate how performer-friendly they are in supporting the performance expected of typical performers. The job descriptions, accountabilities, approach, and appropriateness of goals set for each position are reviewed against the organizational vision, strategy, and business unit goals. Studies address customer product and services demands, the business production and services cycle, organizational revenue

Table 9-6. Process improvement actions.

Actions	Intervention Impact
Goal Setting and Continuous Improvement	Future or "should" performance established to support the business needs of the organization identified against the baseline of current or "is" performance. Goals and continuous improvement results are measured as part of the HPI scorecard.
Policies and Procedures	Policies are guidelines on what is to be done and why. Procedures are the specific steps to be followed in performing a task. Policies and procedures are required documentation for performers to complete a task to standard efficiently with minimum errors.
Position Workload, Tasks, and Accountabilities	The level of tasks and duties assigned to a position that contribute to the goals and success of the organization. Provides clarity on who performs what tasks to eliminate redundancies. Performance expectations are determined by the level of production required within a specified time period.
Staffing Models and Levels	The optimal types and numbers of positions needed during specified periods of time to support the business.
Work-Flow Streamlining	The alignment and processing of steps to complete a task to standard. Decreasing the number of moving parts increases speed, reliability, and quality.
Systems and Technology Reengineering	The analysis and change of processes, models, and operational and human systems to determine how to improve the efficiency and effectiveness of products and services.

goals, and customer service standards. The process consultants recommend changes to staffing levels and work-flow steps for positions within the business unit. They design tools that support the recommended changes. Examples of some of these tools include easy step guides, changes to systems screens, and staffing model guides for managers that are intuitive to the performer and leverage the work performed by the performance improvement sub-team and the skills-and-knowledge sub-team.

Performance Improvement Actions

The performance improvement sub-team provides competencies in the design and development of actions and tools that improve performance through changes in the work environment (table 9-7). The performance consultant looks for sources of employee stress and links changes in leadership selection, development, and coaching to build a workplace supportive of high performance. Possibly the greatest effect on employee performance is made by transforming technical managers into leaders. It is the leader who selects, develops, motivates, rewards, and recognizes employees. The ability of the leader to build a dynamic, high-performing team is a fundamental requirement for breakthroughs in performance. Some of the tools created by the performance improvement team include leadership performance models, executive and leadership development programs, performance management systems, coaching guides, recognition programs, and selection guides.

Skills-and-Knowledge Improvement Actions

The skills-and-knowledge improvement sub-team develops facilitator-led, e-learning delivery, and knowledge-based programs and tools (table 9-8). The tools include electronic and paper-based job aids, leader-led skill refresher modules, structured on-the-job training, and development planning guides. Other tools include intranet knowledge-sharing sites, on-line best practices chat rooms, and online documentation warehousing. These actions are often expensive to develop and implement and are always integrated into the team's process and performance improvement actions.

As the actions and menu of tools for each action are developed and customized to the intervention, it is important to test them before full implementation. This testing involves performer tryouts and field pilots. Early in the development of actions and tools, performance consultants should identify a half-dozen typical performers. These typical performers try out the basic design and usefulness of each tool to see if they help them achieve performance expectations. The tryout occurs in exactly the same environment, with the same equipment and resources that other typical performers experience in their daily work routines. The team leader conducts

Table 9-7. Performance improvement actions.

	Action	Intervention Impact
Client Actions	Leadership	The competencies and behaviors demonstrated by leaders on the job that create a high-performing work environment, communication, coaching, teamwork, and motivated and skilled employees.
	Ownership of Performance Problems and Solutions	The personal involvement and willingness of a client to share responsibility for the implementation of performance improvement interventions.
	Provision of Resources	Provides resources, tools, equipment, facilities, and personnel needed for the quality implementation of HPI interventions.
Human Resources Actions	Performance Management	The system that helps managers and performers work together to set goals, establish accountabilities, identify strengths and weaknesses in competencies, receive performance coaching, financial rewards, and nonfinancial recognition based on results achieved.
	Employee Selection Model	The hiring of the right person for the position based on a profile of core competencies, experiences, and behaviors needed to achieve performance expectations. Selection is one of the most critical leadership accountabilities that affects the ability of performers and business units to achieve target level results.
	Employee Retention Model	The combination of proper selection, performance management, leadership, development, reward and recognition, and a supportive workplace that creates strong employee satisfaction and loyalty. An essential component of quality results sustainable over time is the ability of leaders to retain a highly skilled, motivated workforce. High turnover is a strong barrier to client business results and the HPI department's success.
	Leadership Development	The assessment of strengths and weaknesses against core leadership competencies and the planned development actions to improve leader skills and behaviors. The lack of leadership development programs supported by executive management is a major barrier to performance improvement. Actions include external programs with peer groups, internal programs, coaching and mentoring models.
	Work Environment	The performance consultant identifies barriers to performance and, with the support of the client, builds actions and tools to eliminate or reduce the effect of the barrier on employee or organizational performance. Enhancers, or activities that help employees perform to standard, are maintained or strengthened. It takes the combination of process improvement, skills-and-knowledge improvement, and client and HR actions in performance improvement to change the work environment so employees can make breakthroughs in performance.

the performer tryout with performance consultants serving as evaluators to determine what works and doesn't work. The tryout serves as a quality check on the design and usefulness of the tools under development.

Field pilot tests for each action and menu of tools are conducted near the end of the action development cycle of the implementation phase. A

Table 9-8. Skills-and-knowledge improvement actions.

Action	Intervention Result
Training Curricula	Skill- and knowledge-building programs and performance support tools that build employee competencies required to achieve the performance expectations of the position.
Workplace Development	Structured learning conducted in the business and coached by the manager to achieve required competencies and expected results.
Tools, Job Aids, and Templates	Performance support tools developed as a set of quick steps or knowledge needed to perform a task to standard.
E-Learning Solutions	Programs and tools that are developed, updated, and delivered to employees through Intranet, Web, or disk access using PCs. These tools include wizards, reference libraries, key forms, and procedures that are essential for employees to achieve expectations.
Knowledge Management	Online access to current policies, procedures, documents, and best practices that give the employee the necessary information to improve individual performance.

representative sample of typical performers and exemplary performers tests the actions and tools against the reality of the client's performance expectations. Testing occurs in the performers' work environment. Actions from the three areas of HPI—skills and knowledge, process improvement, and performance improvement—are tested as one integrated solution. The team leader, sub-team leaders, evaluator, and subject matter experts conduct the pilot and assess results. Each sub-team quickly redesigns the plan to finalize actions and tools. The team leader and evaluator share the results of the pilot test with the client. They review what worked well and not so well in closing the client's performance gap(s). The team and the client agree upon any needed changes in the intervention actions and plan. The final timeline for implementation is completed.

Action Step 4: Apply Your Knowledge to a Case Study

 This case study should be used as an example of how select actions from tables 9-6, 9-7, and 9-8 are applied by a consulting team working on employee retention. Harry, the consulting team leader, spends a couple of weeks after the contract meeting with Susan, his client, finalizing the implementation plan. Harry works closely with George, one of Susan's direct reports, and his line co-leader and with the sub-team leaders to prepare for an implementation plan review meeting with Susan. Having a line co-leader for this type of intervention is important to Harry because most actions to improve retention involve changes to the work environment and client behaviors and skills.

At the implementation plan review meeting, Harry and George present the final plan to Susan for approval. Susan is generally supportive of the plan and asks questions about the purpose and actions of the three sub-teams. She has some difficulty understanding how the activities of the three teams and her business unit will be orchestrated. George reassures Susan that her responsibilities as the co-leader include the coordination of the team's activities with Susan's business managers.

Susan is satisfied but raises another concern that was last expressed at the data collection meeting. She is concerned about the amount of time and resources it may take to develop, test, and implement the actions of the three sub-teams. She wonders why the consulting team can't just move ahead with the training that the skills-and-improvement team will build. The other two sub-teams can wait to see how well the training works and then build the actions and tools that her unit will absolutely need. Susan suggests that this approach will speed up support for her unit while keeping down expenses.

Harry maintains his composure at the unexpected direction that Susan wants to take with this intervention. He counters by reminding Susan how well the process has worked so far, the need to follow the next phase to give her a complete solution, and how this will save her resources and improve performance over the long haul. Susan counters with a variation of her same concerns. After several minutes of this type of discussion, Harry sees that although he is making some headway with the logic of his position, Susan is holding firm. Harry offers a compromise that maintains the integrity of the process but moves the intervention forward. Susan agrees and they decide to prioritize the "big six" actions. One of these actions involves skills-and-knowledge improvement. Harry makes sure that the other five are important process and performance improvement actions that the consulting team believes will move the retention initiative in the right direction.

The big six actions are clustered around the main barriers to employee performance identified during the data collection phase of the HPI process that most contribute to turnover. The big six actions are

+ pay and incentives
+ workload and staffing
+ sales and service methods

+ leadership practices
+ supportive work environment
+ training.

Pay and Incentives

Harry recommends updating benchmarking studies on pay competitiveness and incentive design and then sharing that information with performers. The results of the benchmarking indicate that adjustments to pay ranges and individual compensation are appropriate to be competitive. Incentive design is reviewed for appropriateness of target-level goals, complexity, and amount of reward. Incentives are also reviewed for motivating performers to appropriate sales and service behaviors in keeping with the vision, values, and strategy of the organization. Performance consultants identify a sample of performers and seek their input on proposed changes to the organization's compensation practices.

Workload and Staffing

The consulting team carries out a workload study for each position in the business unit along with a staffing model review. Harry presents findings to Susan that indicate that, in Susan's unit, there are too few employees during peak client demand. Harry recommends adjusting the workload to remove distractions that preclude employees from providing excellent sales and service support to clients. The consulting team creates new job descriptions and a revised staffing model for Susan's division. These changes provide performers with the staffing and position accountabilities appropriate for providing high-quality customer service and the time for attending training sessions.

Sales and Service Methods

The data gathered from Susan's business unit indicates that sales and service methods are inflexible and prescribed for performers without the ability to adapt to the needs and wants of the client. The organization appears to want employees to sell for the sake of selling rather than focusing on client needs. The consulting team recommends revising sales and service policies and procedures to emphasize needs-based selling. Harry strongly emphasizes to Susan that her leaders must coach their employees on needs-based selling techniques with clients.

Leadership Practices

Harry discusses with Susan the importance of coaching her leaders about how to implement the performance management system effectively and on using coaching and recognition techniques with their team members. These actions improve retention barriers associated with late salary reviews, poor reinforcement, and lack of coaching for employee development. The consulting team identifies poor leadership practices as one of the primary reasons employees leave the organization. With Susan's approval, the consulting team develops a revised performance management system, communication, and coaching guides. Performance consultants talk through how to use the guides and coaching tips with Susan and her direct reports. Susan's senior managers coach their managers using the guides and established performance expectations on changing leadership behaviors.

Supportive Work Environment

The consulting team works with the help desk in enhancing systems, service quality standards, and behaviors. The team develops job aids for technical and complex issues routinely facing performers as actions to better support client problem resolution. A marketing specialist is on the consulting team and agrees to provide employees with more frequent and broader access to organizational communication. Marketing also forwards materials to performers on new or revised products and services before the materials are distributed to the customers. Previously mentioned changes in staffing model levels, position accountabilities, leader behaviors, sales methods, and pay contribute to improving the work environment and improving employee retention.

Training

The consulting team creates competency models for leaders and performers. The consulting team uses these models and the revised job descriptions to buy or internally develop training where there is an actual gap in required versus current skills. For Susan's business unit, the team recommends mandatory leadership training linked to work environment barriers to retention for all managers within the unit. The consulting team, in partnership with Susan's direct reports, develops sales and service refresher training to be delivered in the workplace, and the unit's managers prepare for their facilitation roles.

Harry and George work with Susan and her other direct reports to implement these actions. The consulting team implements the big six actions and the tools that support them seamlessly as a single, unified intervention. For the first two quarters, there is little discernible change in retention as these actions are being implemented. Harry and George meet frequently with Susan and brief her on the progress of the implementation and on the observable changes in the work environment that are occurring. In the third quarter, employee turnover decreases at an annualized rate of 5 percent. The team and the client continue to work on institutionalizing the improvement actions. In the fourth quarter, turnover drops 15 percent to its lowest level in organizational history. The expense and opportunity cost savings are calculated at $1.5 million annually.

What is the reaction within the organization when these results are announced? The high-quality, bottom-line results elevate the HPI department's standing in the organization. Clients begin to see it as a department that adds value, is part of the core business of the organization, and is a stakeholder in the future of the organization.

Progress Milestones

Chapters 7, 8, and 9 provided you with a template on how to develop and implement the phases of the HPI process. These chapters also gave you a detailed understanding of how to integrate the HPI functions using the new process to solve client performance problems. All of the concepts and tools you previously learned in the partnering and contracting, and gathering data and assessment phases of the HPI process culminate in the implementation of intervention actions. In chapter 9 you specifically examined the intervention phase of the HPI process and learned tips on how to organize the structure and roles of the consulting team. You learned that the cross-functional consulting team must include practitioners from the various functions since complete solutions to performance problems require skills and knowledge, process, and performance improvement actions. The chapter presents the various intervention actions that may be needed for complete solutions to your client's performance problems.

Chapter 10 provides you the opportunity to carefully examine how HPI departments will develop a comprehensive measurement model appropriate for the complexity and scope of performance improvement interventions. The HPI scorecard is a critical component of the HPI process. This chapter gives you an approach and a series of balanced measures to consider in adapting your measurement model to the needs of your clients and your HPI department.

Key Points of This Chapter

✔ Partner with a highly credible client with the willingness to partner, own, and commit resources for an HPI intervention. The intervention must be manageable, of reasonably short duration, and within the consulting competencies and capabilities of the HPI team.

✔ Build an HPI consulting cross-functional team comprising all of the performance improvement functions and appropriate service partners in the organization.

✔ Invest in the coaching and technical competencies of the more experienced consultants so they can serve as mentors for others on the consulting team.

✔ Anticipate and deal with client resistance to the time and expense of conducting an HPI intervention through continuous education and communication.

✔ Position this first intervention as a learning experience for the HPI department and the client. Be sure to carefully manage the expectations of the client and the consulting team.

✔ Capture the lessons learned and frequently debrief the team and the client on what is working well and not so well.

✔ Be proud of completing the first intervention and celebrate success with the client. Use this first success as a springboard for more business within the organization.

10

Measuring HPI Success With the HPI Scorecard

easurement: Do you think it is a necessary evil or an indispensable ally? Although HPI practitioners often say that measurement is critical to the profession, many do little in the way of determining the value added to the clients' units by the HPI department. Each HPI function represented in the department tends to approach measurement differently, often with tools that are designed to measure single-event solutions. Many of the HPI functions do not have the process models or measurement tools to provide clients with reliable data and analyses on gaps and gains in performance. Human performance improvement practitioners from these functions are often faced with the need to quantify results but have little in the way of measures that are credible to their clients. This situation isn't the client's problem. Nothing will change until *you* make measurement an important competency and performance expectation for each consultant and a way of doing business for the HPI department.

Measurement is changing from a focus on measures appropriate for single-event solutions to a balanced scorecard. The scorecard approach provides you with a more comprehensive set of measures for measuring the success of your HPI interventions. This chapter advocates the use of an HPI scorecard and provides a model for you to use when customizing your own measurement process.

Action Steps to Measure Your Success in Improving Performance

1. Gather information on measurement models and tools used in the marketplace and within your organization. Use external partners to help gather measurement best practices in the marketplace.
2. Build and pilot test the HPI scorecard in partnership with a client on a performance consulting intervention.

3. Identify the components of an HPI scorecard. Sell practitioners and clients on its benefits.
4. Develop the HPI scorecard, drawing upon the best practices from the unique measurement models of all the functions.
5. Identify potential problems with HPI measurement and plan actions to overcome these barriers to the successful implementation of the HPI scorecard.

Action Step 1: Gather Information on Measurement Models and Tools

Table 10-1 lists some major contributors to the field of measurement of HPI interventions. With the exception of the balanced scorecard, they represent the foundation of measurement provided by the skills and knowledge improvement functions of training and instructional systems design. The

Table 10-1. Significant contributors to measurement.

Individual	Contribution
Stufflebeam (1988) & Guba (1989)	Developed a measurement model for the evaluation of basic skills training by investigating the following: • Are client's goals convergent or divergent? • Are program resources adequate and used well? • Are program development and implementation aligned with program goals? • Are program goals being met?
Robert Stake (1991)	Developed formative evaluation: • self or peer evaluation • content expert evaluation • learner tryout • field test
Donald Kirkpatrick (1994)	Developed summative evaluation: • reaction • learning • performance • results
Jack Phillips (1997)	Added a fifth level of summative evaluation: return on investment
Kaplan & Norton (1996)	Created a balanced scorecard of measures: • customer perspective • financial perspective • innovation, growth, and learning perspective • business process perspective

Handshaw, LaBonte, & Robinson, 1998.

balanced scorecard provides the framework for performance consultants to build an HPI scorecard that integrates success measures from all of the HPI functions.

Table 10-2 lists the approach to measurement often used by practitioners from selected HPI functions. The information in this table compares and contrasts several different measurement models that may be used by practitioners in the new HPI department. Some of the HPI functions found in many organizations are omitted from the list because they do not have a measurement model that is universally adopted by its practitioners.

Training Measures

Training is a single-event performance solution with success measures that are often limited by trainers to evaluating its effect on acquisition and application of skills and knowledge. Measurement in training usually involves the four levels of the Kirkpatrick model by Donald Kirkpatrick (1994) and level 5 created by Jack Phillips (1997). Trainers almost always capture level 1 data, and many perform level 2 evaluation as well. Far fewer capture level 3 data. Probably no more than 5 percent of HPI practitioners even attempt some type of financial measurement that resembles level 4 or 5.

Table 10-2. Selected HPI functions' measurement models.

HPI Function	Measurement Model
Training (Kirkpatrick Model)	• Reaction: Determines how participants value the training by completing an end of program or activity questionnaire • Learning: determines if participants meet program learning objectives often through pre- and post-testing • Behavioral application: determines if there is a change in job performance 60 to 90 days after program or activity completion • Business results: determines financial impact using measures such as increased customer satisfaction and sales and cost savings • Return-on-investment: quantifies cost-benefit as the relationship between the amount of investment to conduct the activity versus amount of return (Phillips, 1997)
Quality	Measures process improvements such as cycle times, amount of rework, reduced turnaround, decreased error rate, and increased production due to revised work flow
Organization Development	Measures the impact of leadership development and cultural change through satisfaction surveys and degree of change on the job usually using levels 1 and 3 of the Kirkpatrick model
Performance Improvement	Typically measures the effects of work-environment changes and operational increases in productivity on business unit results using levels 3 and 4 of the Kirkpatrick model

Often from the client's perspective, level 1 and level 2 data has little meaning for their business. Say, for example, that participants' training evaluations show that they were happy with the training and rated the facilitator a 4.7 on a 5.0 scale. With a mean score of 90 percent, the posttest scores were 30 percent higher than the pretest scores. The client may even comment on the gain in learning. One question remains unanswered: How do these scores affect the client's bottom line? Do these scores mean that employee productivity and business results will improve and be reflected on the bottom line? Will service quality increase? Are these increases sustainable?

Clients often begin to get interested in quantifiable data from levels 3, 4, and 5. The complexity and skill required to successfully perform these levels of measurement may deter some trainers from attempting to use these measures. Others find it difficult to explain to clients the linkage between training solutions and financial impact measures, which depend on a number of variables beyond the trainer's control. These financial measures of performance are better applied in process and performance improvement interventions for which the multiple variables that influence these complex measures can be manipulated.

In summary, the Kirkpatrick model has served the training community well. It has provided the training profession with a model that enjoys universal acceptance. The Kirkpatrick model does not have the breadth of measures and tools required to support adequately the measurement requirements of more complex HPI interventions.

Quality and OD Measures

The quality and OD functions within the HPI department offer measurement tools that fill some of the gaps in measures needed for HPI interventions. Quality tools are used in measuring gains in productivity, efficiency, and cost-benefit from process improvements. Organizational development measures support the correlations among employee loyalty, customer loyalty, and increases in revenue growth and profitability. Organizational development measures also gauge the effects of changes in leader's skills and behaviors on organizational and business unit results.

Performance Improvement Measures

One of the great contributions of the new HPI process is its focus on measurement. Measurement is a topic of discussion, preparation, and execution throughout the partnering, data collection, and implementation phases of the HPI process. During the partnering phase, the consultant facilitates client discussions and establishes a contract outlining goals and broadly defined success measures. The contract also contains specific types of data collection methods, role clarity, and accountabilities of the client and consultant in applying measurement tools.

In the data collection phase, sources and methods are linked to target performance measures. The phase is designed so that the data collected supports the success measures used in measuring the effect of the HPI intervention. The scorecard measures are finalized at the data-reporting meeting with the client.

When clients agree on actions to close performance gaps, they also agree in the implementation contract to the specific measures that become the HPI scorecard. The rich menu of measurement tools from the various HPI functions support the actions outlined in the client contract. The full power of the measurement model is applied during the implementation phase to measure the effect of the intervention on the client's business results.

Action Step 2: Build and Pilot Test the HPI Scorecard

What the new HPI department needs is a set of measurement tools that supports the complex business and performance needs facing most organizations today. These performance problems often require interventions and measurement tools that integrate performance, process, and skills-and-knowledge actions. A balanced scorecard model (Kaplan & Norton, 1996) allows measurement of this type of client performance problems. The HPI scorecard is a comprehensive measurement model that is aligned with the new HPI process and the strategic direction of the organization. The scorecard provides the tools needed to establish measurement standards and expectations for clients and the HPI department. Table 10-3 lists some of the benefits of the scorecard.

Action Step 3: Identify the Components of an HPI Scorecard

General scorecard measures apply to all functions within the HPI department and all phases of the HPI process. General scorecard measures may include the following:

+ client and employee satisfaction
+ financial effect
+ performance and process improvement
+ skills-and-knowledge improvement.

Client and Employee Satisfaction

Determining client and employee satisfaction is important to maintaining and strengthening relationships with key partners. These measures (table

Table 10-3. Benefits of the HPI scorecard.

Organizational Benefits	HPI Department Benefits
Demonstrates what is different about the new HPI process, products, and services	Translates the priorities in the HPI process to each performance consultant
Permits the tracking of strategic and tactical gains in performance improvement	Links consultant performance and the use of the new HPI process to future career opportunities and compensation
Gives clients and the HPI department information on how to continuously improve HPI products and services in support of business needs	Provides a great motivational tool for the HPI leader to use for influencing behavioral change and growth with new and existing HPI practitioners
Provides complete measures of improved performance	Serves as a framework for pulling together the best of the models from the HPI functions into a menu of measurement tools
Shorter-term financial measures and longer-term operational measures become essential drivers of business unit and organizational performance	Helps the HPI leader translate the vision, values, and strategy of the new HPI department into a tangible reality
	Moves the HPI department into a new level of credibility and importance
	Demonstrates to clients why continued support of the HPI department is in the organization's best interest

10-4) provide the client and consultant with the opportunity to give objective feedback on the quality of the relationship and HPI products and services. The data from these satisfaction measures is critical to the continuous improvement efforts of the HPI department. In designing these measurement tools, the HPI leader and consultants need to know the following:

+ What are the business and performance needs of clients that are driven by satisfaction measures?
+ What are client and employee satisfiers that should be measured within the organization?
+ What is the link between employee and customer satisfaction and business results?

Financial Impact

The HPI department needs to demonstrate that it is a contributor and stakeholder to current and future financial success (table 10-5). The influence of the HPI department on business growth and profitability is measured by its partnering with clients on interventions that help the organization increase

146

Table 10-4. A sample list of client satisfaction measures.

Success Measure	Achieve Target	Exceed Target	Method
Client Satisfaction	80% or 4.0 rating	90% or 4.5 rating	Client survey with 5.0 scale, semiannual service shops, and telephone surveys
Business Unit Employee Satisfaction	80% or 4.0 rating; absenteeism down 5% monthly; turnover down 10% annualized rate	90% or 4.5 rating; absenteeism down 8% monthly; turnover down 12% annualized rate	Annual employee survey, monthly attendance data, quarterly retention report
Client Partnering	Monthly proactive contact with all clients; meet client expectations on frequency, quality of meetings, responsiveness to needs, problem resolution	Frequency and quality of meetings, communication, and support that delights the client	Client HPI satisfaction survey; HPI leader-client meeting feedback

its profitable revenue and realize operational efficiencies. The HPI department must demonstrate financially sound management of its resources. This section of the scorecard includes financial measures that start with answering the following questions:

 ✦ How does the HPI department contribute to the financial performance of the organization and the client's business unit?
 ✦ What are the financial measures that are supported by the client and the chief financial officer?
 ✦ How is the scorecard blended into the client's existing financial metrics?

Table 10-5. A sample list of financial effectiveness measures.

Success Measure	Achieve Target	Exceed Target	Method
Return on investment	ROI of 2 within 12 months of intervention	ROI of 3 within 12 months of intervention	Scorecard ROI template; client intervention contract
Turnover/Retention	Business unit client retention increases 5% by year-end with $600M in cost savings and $300M increased sales	Business unit client retention increases 7% by year-end with $700M in cost savings and $500M increased sales	Client household retention report; household sales report
Decreased Expenses	Meet all client contract goals with expenses 1% under intervention budget	Exceed client expectations on contract goals with expenses 3% under intervention budget	HPI budget report; intervention expense tracking

Performance and Process Improvement

The scorecard provides measurement methods and tools for interventions that support the client's need for credible performance improvement measures (table 10-6). This section of the scorecard integrates a variety of methods and tools from the HPI functions. Building this section of the scorecard starts with answering the following questions:

- ✦ How do consultants using the HPI process add value to the organization and the client's business unit?
- ✦ What results from the new process differentiate the HPI department from the previous HPI functions?
- ✦ What HPI products and services do clients support measuring?
- ✦ What is the effect of HPI products and services on organizational and client goals?

Skills-and-Knowledge Improvement

This section of the scorecard deals with improving the skills and knowledge of the client's team members as one component of increasing organizational performance (table 10-7). It also focuses on the competencies and individual

Table 10-6. A sample list of performance and process improvement measures.

Success Measure	Achieve Target	Exceed Target	Method
Intervention Goals	Meet all client goals in contract; client business unit results achieving targets by year-end; 5% increase in completed interventions	Exceed client goals in contract; client breakthroughs in business unit and employee results make it a trendsetter in the organization; 7% increase in completed interventions	HPI process contract; client survey at end of intervention; business unit and organization business goals achievement report; scorecard measures
Project Management	Project deliverables completed on time and within budget; cost of production reduced $5/unit/day; less than 5% rework within 1 month of completion	Project completed 10% ahead of schedule, cost of production reduced $8/unit/day; less than 1% rework within 1 month of completion	Client contract and goals; project planning matrix; scorecard measures; client satisfaction survey; business unit cost report
Product and Services Innovation	Adapt existing HPI products and services to client business needs; create new products and services that close the client's performance gaps to the client's satisfaction	Exceed client expectations by rapidly building new tools that are qualitatively superior in helping the client generate results	Client quarterly satisfaction survey; improved turnaround time for intervention actions; number of new ideas/tools recommended and used in client interventions

growth needed by each HPI practitioner in supporting the performance needs of the HPI department. Some of the questions answered in this section of the scorecard include the following:

- ✦ Is the organization investing properly in the skills and performance of its employees?
- ✦ Are employee business results increasing through improvement of skills and knowledge?
- ✦ Do HPI practitioners have the skills and knowledge that are required for their new consulting roles in supporting client business needs?

Scorecard Function-Specific Measures

In addition to the general measures that cut across the organization and the HPI department, function-specific measures are also identified. Each area within the HPI department has specific success measures unique to that particular function. For example, compensation and employment have existing models and tools that support improving performance as part of the solutions they provide to clients on a daily basis (tables 10-8 and 10-9). The key

Table 10-7. A sample list of skills-and-knowledge improvement measures.

Success Measure	Achieve Target	Exceed Target	Method
Practitioner Competencies	Each individual has a development plan; attains proficiency in one new consulting competency per quarter; demonstrates proficiency in these competencies within 12 months of completing the performance consulting workshop	Attain proficiency in several consulting competencies per quarter; coaches other consultants and may serve as a team leader; within 18 months of completing the performance consulting workshop attains application level of proficiency	Consulting workshop evaluation, on-the-job application and coaching; performance management; client satisfaction survey
Participant Satisfaction	4.0 on 5.0 scale: program content, goal achievement, and delivery	4.5 on 5.0 scale	End of program questionnaire
Participant Learning	Attain 80% pass rate	Attain 90% pass rate	Criterion-based pre- and posttests
Application	80% transfer of skills on the job; increased skills and results observable	90% transfer of skills on the job; improved skills contributes to business unit results	90-day postintervention, on the job surveys of peers, managers, and the participant

Table 10-8. Compensation function measures.

Success Measure	Achieve Target	Exceed Target	Method
Pay for Performance	Total annual compensation expense as % of payroll equal to peer organizations; ratio of revenue-to-expense achieves client goal	Total annual compensation expense as % of payroll less than peer organizations; ratio of revenue-to-expense exceeds client expectations	Monthly revenue and expense reports; quarterly client satisfaction survey
Recognition	Employee satisfaction improves by 3% annualized—tracked quarterly	Employee satisfaction improves by 5% annualized—tracked quarterly	Employee satisfaction survey
Performance and Salary Reviews	92% submitted by due date; 95% accuracy	95% submitted by due date; 99% accuracy	Appraisal schedule; HR policies and procedures

is to link the functional and general measures so that they support measurements of the total effect of interventions on the client's business. It is the responsibility of the HPI leader and consulting team leaders to ensure that the general and function-specific measures are implemented in parallel and are mutually supporting.

Action Step 4: Develop the HPI Scorecard

The HPI leader and managers meet to link the organization's strategic direction and the HPI department vision with a scorecard of performance measures. The HPI management team works together, often with an external partner, to build the scorecard and blend the best models and tools from each function. All the functions contribute, but it is important that the managers of quality, OD, and training bring their unique measurement tools to the meeting. The active involvement of each consultant is also important so that resistance is minimized to using a scorecard of balanced financial and nonfinancial measures. This collaboration of all HPI team functions is essential if individual consultants are expected to adopt a new scorecard approach to measurement. The main steps for developing an HPI scorecard are the following:

+ Align the vision of the HPI department with the vision of the organization, balancing short- and long-term measures with the organization's strategic direction.
+ Define the measures that are critical to the success of the vision and business strategies.

Table 10-9. A sample list of employment function measures.

Success Measures	Achieve Target	Exceed Target	Methods
Quality of Hires	Meet client standards in new-hire skills and behaviors; reduce employee relations problems annually by 5%	Exceed client expectations in new-hire quality; reduce employee relations problems annually by 10%	Quarterly client survey; selection profile data; employee relations log
Recruiter Productivity	Eight new hires per month meeting all position qualifications; reduce time to fill monthly quota by 2 days each month	Minimum of 10 fully qualified new hires monthly; reduce fill time by 3 days each month	Position fill rate, client satisfaction survey
New Employee Orientation	90% attend within 30 days of hire, participant and client satisfaction ratings of 4.0	95% attend within 30 days of hire, participant and client satisfaction ratings of 4.5	New employee orientation attendance records; participant survey; client satisfaction survey

✦ Build a menu of tools for the organization-wide general measures and function-specific department measures. Link them to each category of actions in the intervention phase.

✦ Test the tools in several business units with consulting interventions in progress and with the active support of your clients.

✦ The HPI leader calls an HPI department meeting to work through the model, obtain recommendations for change, and solicit ideas on how to institutionalize the new scorecard.

✦ Integrate the scorecard into the department's performance management and compensation systems as well as the leader-coaching schedule.

✦ Integrate the HPI scorecard into the department's performance consulting and measurement workshops. Each consulting team implements the scorecard by working closely with its clients.

Action Step 5: Identify Potential Problems With HPI Measurement

Often performance consultants are amazed to discover that some clients are reluctant to measure the effects of an intervention. Even though clients have a variety of financial and nonfinancial measures they use daily, the thought of measuring a consulting intervention does not generate much enthusiasm. Why? Many clients may want a quick fix. They may believe that taking the time to measure improved performance isn't worth the time or expense. Other clients may question the relevance or credibility of the traditional, single-event measures that are in use. Sometimes clients are nervous about committing to a measurement plan that is conducted by someone outside of their business unit.

The performance consultant's job is to help the client see that the HPI scorecard is not a burdensome addition to an already demanding schedule. Measurement must appear to be seamless with current business practices for widespread client support. It is advantageous to align the model with organizational and business unit measures whenever the opportunity presents itself. This approach also avoids putting the consultant in the awkward position of relying on measures that are irrelevant to the client.

It isn't just clients who may resist the measurement of HPI interventions. Often, HPI leaders find resistance from within the HPI department to changing the approach to measurement or doing any measurement beyond level 1 participant reaction. Anticipating these problems and identifying actions to resolve them as the scorecard is being planned helps ease the change to new scorecard measures. Table 10-10 presents some of these problems and potential solutions to working through the change to an HPI scorecard.

Table 10-10. Troubleshooting measurement problems.

Problem	Potential Solution
Consultant or team lacks skill and knowledge	Set expectations that all consultants attend performance consulting and measurement workshops, use the scorecard, and receive coaching
Lack of client ownership and client is resistant to change	Build greater client involvement in measurement decisions throughout the process; establish joint ownership at very beginning of client relationship; ensure that measures have CFO and client credibility
Inadequte resources—time, money, technology and available people	Establish priorities for allocation of resources based on potential client impact; share resource burden with clients; select new hires to fill gaps in measurement competencies
The HPI department has a weakly designed measurement model	Hire an external partner to help create a new scorecard or revise the existing scorecard; follow steps in creating the HPI scorecard; focus on measures with greatest support from the CFO and clients
Poor communication and understanding on the purpose, value, and approach to measuring HPI interventions	Build a marketing and communication plan; use organization's existing media to maximum advantage; make presentations to client's departments and HPI department; seek endorsement by senior management

How can the HPI team avoid such problems before they occur? The answer lies in partnering effectively with clients. Before beginning the transition to an HPI scorecard, be sure to have the active support of the organization's chief financial officer (CFO) and main clients. These executives are critical to the success of the HPI scorecard and should become the scorecard champions of the organization. The CFO must support the financial and quantitative measures. Senior line clients help with testing and implementing the scorecard in consulting interventions. Remember that with most clients, simplicity and ease of understanding in measurement are virtues. So before investing heavily in theoretical, statistically heavy methodologies and tools, check with the client. Before finalizing the scorecard, be sure to review it with the client. It is easier to sell the HPI team on the merits of changing to the scorecard if they see this level of client support.

Communication is listed in table 10-10 as a potential problem that the HPI leader must address with clients and consultants. No stone can be left unturned in communicating the need, purpose, and value of the scorecard. The HPI leader communicates what will be different for the client and for the HPI department when the scorecard is designed and implemented. The communication plan includes explaining the critical success factors, clarifying roles, and the content and uses of the scorecard. The client and HPI team members are reassured that the model is not burdensome, that it is not overly time-consuming, and that it adds value to the business unit. The plan involves a protracted campaign using internal newsletters, video, client meetings, and testimonials from line managers.

Progress Milestones

Chapter 10 presents the argument that it takes leadership, resources of time and money, and commitment of clients and the HPI team to build an integrated measurement model. This is particularly challenging when some HPI practitioners have operated in functions with activity data as their sole measure of success. Yet there are often practitioners from the functions of quality, ISD, and OD with competencies and experience in measurement. Finance and market research internal partners have measurement and analytical competencies. You may identify several of the more experienced measurement practitioners from these functions and recruit them to serve in the role of evaluators. You can use the evaluators as internal consultants and team leaders for building the measurement model and establishing a baseline of measurement competency in the new HPI department.

From reading chapter 10 you already recognize that gaining consensus within the HPI functions on measurement may not be as difficult as gaining client commitment to use these measures. Although clients are held accountable to a variety of measures and believe it is good business to do so, building and implementing performance improvement measures often requires a hard sell. Your success depends on establishing a partnership of clients, internal partners, and the HPI team to implement a highly credible scorecard. The HPI process you have built for your organization is not complete without a measurement model that is supported by key HPI stakeholders in your organization. This chapter contains recommendations, tools, and approaches that you can adapt to your unique HPI process, organizational strategies, and business needs.

 ## Key Points of This Chapter

✔ Build upon the existing measurement models used by HPI functions and internal partners in your organization. Use an external partner to pull in best practices in measurement from the marketplace.

✔ Assign each member of the HPI department a baseline of competency in learning and using the new scorecard.

✔ Invest in workshops and coaching with the department's evaluators first. Then, after they gain experience and confidence in the new scorecard, have them facilitate the learning and coaching of other HPI practitioners.

✔ Insist that HPI consultants use measurement skills for the partnering and contracting phase, for the data collection phase (sorting, analyzing, summarizing implications), for client coaching, and for determination of the success of consulting interventions.

✔ The scorecard brings tangible results to the client in that it validates gains in improved performance. Use these successes as communication and marketing opportunities.

✔ Reward and recognize performance consultants for the successful application of the HPI scorecard with clients.

✔ The HPI scorecard evolves and grows with the ongoing success of consulting interventions. The ability of the HPI department to successfully apply the scorecard with clients must evolve and grow as well.

Afterword:
Build Your New Performance Vision

In the 50-year history of the HPI profession a great deal has changed, and yet more change is needed. With all of the books, lectures, conferences, and education on performance improvement, the approach to solving performance problems in many organizations is little changed over the past half-century. In so many organizations today you see the same recurring issues:

+ The HPI functions operate as silos, often with an internal focus rather than a focus on the client's business needs.
+ HPI functions often provide fragmented, incomplete process models and tools for improving performance.
+ HPI functions are often unable to completely support the total performance needs of clients. Practitioners often lack the competencies needed to help clients solve business unit and organizational performance problems. This results in HPI functions and practitioners lacking credibility with clients.
+ There is competition between HPI functions for ownership of the client.
+ HPI functions often lack adequate resources due their lack of measurable results, client credibility, and performance support issues.
+ There is no perceived HPI ownership or stake in the business.
+ There is a growing movement toward client outsourcing for performance support instead of relying on internal HPI capabilities.

What do your clients need? Clients need HPI practitioners to make the evolution from a transactional, internally centered approach to a tactical focus on closing performance gaps and a strategic focus on organizational strategies and goals. Your efforts in aligning process, organizational structure, and performer readiness are critical to the effective transition of your HPI functions into a unified performance improvement department. Your clients need the support of all the HPI functions in the organization if they are to achieve their business goals. You will need to ensure that the HPI department can provide your clients with the following capabilities to meet these needs:

+ models, concepts, and tools that are reliable, fit the organization's business model, and provide complete performance solutions
+ one-stop shopping in an HPI department organized to maximize the strengths of the practitioner's competencies and tools to support the new process
+ timely responsiveness to your client's needs with high-quality, low-cost products and services.

How are we going to close the gap? Often HPI departments are not able to deliver on their client's needs and expectations. What can you do differently as an HPI practitioner to become a credible business partner with your clients? How can the HPI functions eliminate client perceptions of self-interest, the silo mentality, and the lack of focus on the business? As an HPI practitioner, you have a tremendous opportunity to embrace change and become an influence leader, helping clients and the HPI functions work together to create a new, integrated HPI process and department. Everyone in these HPI functions needs to develop a visionary, proactive, innovative, and aggressive approach to the business. This means building relationships with your key clients around their business goals and translating HPI practitioner technical expertise into results. The result is that you should realize a new level of professional growth and credibility with clients, thereby demonstrating the increased value you bring to the organization.

The transformation to a unified HPI department will not be complete until HPI practitioners

+ change their own view of the HPI profession, what they do, and how they do it
+ develop the competencies needed to make the new HPI process a success
+ change, learn, and act faster than the clients and external HPI competitors
+ develop excellent relationship-building skills and behaviors and establish client partnering as the HPI department's foundation for success
+ attract and grow transformational leaders who think, talk, and act as change agents, bringing the HPI functions together with a common vision and purpose
+ implement a process and measurement scorecard that determines the effect of interventions on individual performers, business units, and the organization

✦ build an HPI department structure that provides for the flexible dedication of talent necessary to support client's performance problems

✦ define their roles and competencies and assign the right talent to successfully implement HPI interventions.

What is the future of the HPI profession? In addition to taking control of the reshaping of the HPI profession, there are a number of forces within organizations and in the marketplace that will also shape the future of performance improvement. As the crystal ball comes into focus you may well see the following:

✦ HPI is increasingly integrated into the lines of business. This is the result of line managers adopting performance concepts, language, and realizing the value added to their business units by the new HPI department.

✦ Enterprisewide HPI departments operate as shared services business units with profit center accountabilities for revenue and service quality.

✦ Alliances of business, education, and government take a stronger leadership role in the future of the HPI profession. Corporations and agencies at the state, regional, and national levels are aggressively pursuing professional development, joint HPI ventures, and resource sharing.

✦ Association members vote with their feet and join associations that are able to take strong leadership roles in merger-like associations and in joint membership ventures as customer-focused proponents of performance improvement. Associations actively participate in business, government, and education HPI alliances.

✦ HPI practitioners evolve into performance consultants by learning and applying competencies in technology, consulting, and measurement. These individuals are in high demand in the marketplace, command premium compensation, and have highly mobile competencies and career expectations.

✦ HPI consultants move frequently within organizations between line and HPI positions due to their competencies, experience, and quality results.

✦ The HPI process is adopted as part of the organization's business model. Line managers rotate through HPI assignments to learn the process and competencies to generate improved business results.

You have the opportunity to chart your own course and shape your professional destiny if you are willing to embark on the change to a unified HPI process. Too few HPI professionals have seriously taken up the challenge to change how they operate. If HPI professionals are disenchanted with the state of the profession and the level of credibility established with clients, then this change must begin. These are exciting times for the profession. Make the most of every opportunity to become an agent of change, an active learner, and a developer of new competencies in human performance improvement.

Glossary

Business needs: the operational, quantifiable goals for a business unit or enterprise

Business unit: any department and/or group within an organization that has specific goals and one or more performer groups

Client: the individual accountable for achieving the goals of a business unit with whom the performance consultant partners to improve performance.

Competency model: identifies the skills, knowledge and behaviors required for achieving expectations

Contracting: a workplan between consultant and client that involves defining roles, setting expectations and goals, establishing ground rules on measurement, and meeting/communication agreements

Evaluation: the determination of meaning assigned to the measurement information

Exemplary performer: an individual who consistently achieves superior results by working through barriers to performance in the work environment

Human performance (HPI) function: a combination of practitioners or departments that agree upon a common HPI process and their corresponding roles within that process

Human performance improvement (HPI) process: The process used to systematically partner with clients for purposes of identifying performance problems, analyzing root causes, selecting and designing actions, managing interventions in the workplace, measuring results, and continuously improving performance

Human resources (HR) needs: the employment/selection, reward and recognition, and leadership development support required for the achievement of business and performance needs

Industrial/Organizational psychologist: professionals who conduct job analysis and testing to identify the knowledge, skills, and abilities necessary for employees to perform to organizational expectations

Information technology (IT): the function responsible for designing, re-engineering, and implementing systems and operational applications for the purpose of maximizing performance of business processes

Instructional systems design (ISD): a systematic approach to the design of instruction for the purpose of improving performance through increasing employee skills and knowledge

Intervention: systematically implementing actions to improve human performance by affecting the root causes of performance gaps

Knowledge management: providing performers information and best practices to improve organizational performance by identifying, storing, and disseminating knowledge, data, research studies, policies, procedures, and competitor intelligence

Learning needs: the skills and knowledge required for performers to achieve the performance needs required for their position

Measurement: the act of gathering and assessing quantitative and qualitative data to compare "should" (expected) performance achieved against objective standards and goals

Organization development (OD): an HR function process focused on improving individual and organizational performance by assessing data, building and implementing interventions, and measuring results

Partnering: a long-term, professional relationship of mutual support between consultant and client focused on improving business results

Performance model: identifies expected performance for a new or changing position or a job family of positions

Performance needs: on-the-job requirements, skills, and behaviors for what performers must do if business needs and goals are to be achieved

Process: a series of steps or activities that help a consultant identify actions and produce value-added benefits for a client

Process improvement: a component of human performance improvement involving the analysis, planning, and implementation of best practices and changes to workplace systems, models, and approaches required for the support of client business needs

Stakeholder: a person or team with vested interests in the results of a performance improvement intervention

Strategic planning: establishes organizational strategies for improving business results in revenue growth and profitability through competitive benchmarking and changes in productivity resulting from increased employee and customer satisfaction

Total quality management (TQM): a process improvement methodology that analyzes and measures actions to improve operational effectiveness and efficiencies

Work environment needs: the systems and processes that either enhance or are barriers to desired performance in the workplace

Client Meeting Summary Worksheet

Relationship Manager
or Performance Consultant: _____ Date: _____

Client Name: _____ Department: _____

Location/mail code: _____ email:_____

Telephone/fax numbers: _____   _____

Client's business unit vision/mission: _____
_____
_____
_____

Critical business needs   Potential performance gaps
_____   _____
_____   _____
_____   _____

HPI support previously provided   Status (success level)
_____   _____
_____   _____
_____   _____

Current HPI support   Status
_____   _____
_____   _____
_____   _____

Preferred meeting dates/times: Days_____   Times _____
Meeting frequency: _____weekly   _____biweekly   _____quarterly
Communication routing—who needs to know
____ Relationship managers   ____ HPI department managers
____ Consulting team members   ____ Internal partner:
____ HPI department leader   _____
Notes:

Performance Consulting Job Descriptions

Job Title:	**Performance Consultant I (entry level)**
Department:	**Human Performance Improvement**

Position Overview

Provide performance improvement consulting services to key clients for major projects and initiatives organization-wide or within business units. Apply performance consulting concepts to create and implement interventions that increase the ability of the organization's performers to establish lifetime customer relationships and achieve sustainable competitive advantage. Continuously strive to improve organizational results and efficiencies in the delivery of products and services to customers. Apply knowledge of competitive business and industry trends and skills in consultation, organizational analysis, project management, and instructional product implementation.

The basic application (BA) level of proficiency is required in the competencies of measurement, systems thinking, coaching, and problem solving. The application (A) level of proficiency is required in all other competencies.

Core Competencies/Job Functions

PARTNERING. Identify key clients to establish business relationships. Develop a strategy/plan for how consulting team members will partner with clients. Initiate discussions with clients to review business goals, identify performance gaps, and contract for consulting services. Initiate contact with clients to resolve any blocks that occur during implementation and to obtain feedback on satisfaction with results. Build strong networks with internal service partners to accomplish mutual objectives.

DATA COLLECTION. Partner with clients in selecting interventions with high potential to impact business results. Discuss measurement criteria as a critical step in the assessment strategy. Plan and implement assessment strategies that provide sufficient data for performance improvement interventions. Build a data collection strategy and design appropriate data collection instruments. Organize findings into a report to be used with the client in determining intervention actions.

HPI INTERVENTIONS. Select performance improvement actions that will yield business results. Demonstrate how specific interventions can close performance gaps. Influence managers to support and provide resources for the intervention. Monitor and assess progress on all phases of the intervention. Form a communication plan with the client to share results within the organization.

PROJECT MANAGEMENT. Prepare templates or outlines for intervention or project contracts with clients. Develop clear, concise statements of project goals. Develop project plans and milestones. Anticipate potential problems that may arise and suggest ways to reduce risks. Apply appropriate techniques and tools to monitor progress toward goals. Identify key individuals/groups who need to be kept informed during the project. Apply effective communication methods to keep stakeholders informed. Assess performance against goals using appropriate measures and data.

PERFORMANCE MEASUREMENT. Discuss with clients the process by which performance and operational measures are implemented. Determine the purpose of measurement initiatives, decisions to be made and responsibilities for decision making. Develop a measurement strategy based on an HPI scorecard. Identify existing data collection systems and the types of data they provide for specific interventions. Outline options to client for implementing measurement strategies. Identify stakeholders whose support is required for implementation. Apply basic research statistics and tools in analyzing measurement data for interventions. Engage clients in the interpretation of the findings.

BUSINESS KNOWLEDGE. Assist clients in evaluating competitive and market forces and in determining appropriate action. Suggest to clients how changes in the industry could impact the effectiveness of performer groups. Help clients incorporate information about competitive and industry trends into their business plans. Discuss clients' annual business goals including drivers, strategies for achieving goals, measures of success, and challenges to goal achievement. Provide specific information about business strategies, goals, products and services, processes, and systems when working on an intervention.

SYSTEMS THINKING. Use performance relationship maps with clients to identify interrelationships between operational results, performance results, and internal and external causes. Describe to clients the characteristics, purposes, and limitations of systems that support business goals and required performance. Suggest ways to increase alignment of systems that support performance interventions and achievement of business goals.

FACILITATION. Facilitate meetings with clients to contract for actions. Assist clients in understanding actions needed to achieve business goals. Overcome client resistance to the performance improvement process. Facilitate clarification of the purpose and steps in the performance improvement process used by the performance team. Assist the client and consulting team in reaching consensus on major issues and actions.

COACHING. Discuss with clients the benefits of having coaching and feedback processes in place. Identify and document specific links between business goals and coaching and feedback opportunities. Identify key elements within the work environment that may affect the coaching process. Identify opportunities to provide coaching for specific performance needs to a job family within a department. Describe to clients how to give effective corrective feedback and identify opportunities to provide feedback to individuals/groups for specific performance needs. Explain to clients the purpose and benefit of various coaching and feedback tools and describe how these tools can be used within the organization.

COMMUNICATION. Use appropriate questioning techniques to obtain information from clients. Keep clients and HPI consultants informed of initiatives and activities that will affect them and discuss the implications. Use appropriate techniques to acknowledge messages communicated by clients. Suggest ways that employees' ideas could be acknowledged more effectively.

PROBLEM SOLVING. Apply the problem-solving process to defining the gap between current state and desired state. Identify and differentiate between symptoms and root causes. Use tools (e.g., fishbone diagram) to identify root causes. Outline decision process used in selecting a course of action to solve the problem. Identify criteria for selecting the best possible solution.

Education and Experience

EDUCATION. Bachelor's degree in business, education, organization development, or other appropriate discipline is required. Complete the performance consulting workshop, the performance technology workshop (ISD), and measurement workshop within 6 months of employment.

EXPERIENCE. Six years of consulting or project management or sales and service management is required.

Skills and Abilities

The performance consultant demonstrates skills and knowledge of the following:

+ ability to effectively work as a leader or a member of a consulting team
+ coaching to improve performance and recognition
+ ability to develop and build strong collaborative partnerships
+ ability to conduct needs assessments, collect data, and apply appropriate statistical methods to analyze organizational data and evaluate the effects of performance improvement initiatives
+ understanding of data collection methods and ability to select or design appropriate data collection and evaluation instruments
+ ability to collect, analyze, and interpret information on business and industry trends, organizational strategies, and business goals
+ consulting skills, such as organizational diagnosis, intervention design, and measurement of results against performance goals
+ design and use of technology-based instructional products and performance tools.
+ use of existing and new technologies including different types of operating systems, hardware, software, alternative delivery methods, and electronic support systems
+ project management, including planning, organization, implementation, communication, and measurement of performance against goals
+ ability to effectively convey information, ideas, and conclusions to individuals and groups; seek and acknowledge information, ideas, and conclusions from individuals and groups.

Job Title: Director, Human Performance Improvement
Department: Human Performance Improvement

Position Overview:

Provide comprehensive consulting services focused on organization-wide initiatives to improve performance in support of the organization's mission and business strategies. Manage the planning, coordination, development, and implementation of organizational performance improvement initiatives. Consult on identifying, recommending, implementing, and evaluating the effects of specific performance improvement interventions. Continuously work to improve service levels and efficiencies in the delivery of products and services to clients.

Use key competencies in the areas of performance consulting and leadership. The mastery level of proficiency is required in the competencies of: partnering, HPI interventions, project management, performance measurement, business knowledge, systems thinking, coaching, communication, and problem solving. The application level of proficiency is required for all other competencies.

Core Competencies/Job Functions—Performance Improvement

PARTNERING. Align the priorities and resources of the HPI department with the business needs of executive management. Identify opportunities to expand client partnerships throughout the organization. Propose innovative ways to address client concerns and achieve business goals. Mediate and resolve complex issues that have an impact on clients. Develop collaborative working relationships with key individuals who are reluctant to partner with you. Coach and mentor others in how to strategically build client partnerships. Provide coaching on how to partner with clients in contracting for interventions.

DATA COLLECTION. Plan and implement assessment strategies with clients who provide sufficient information for performance improvement. Tasks include the development of a data collection plan and the design of appropriate data collection instruments. Organize findings into reports to be used in decision making.

HPI INTERVENTIONS. Assess the extent to which a given performance improvement intervention is likely to address the root causes of performance gaps and provide the client with alternatives. When goals are unattainable, clearly indicate this position and create alternatives for the client. Form plans to overcome resistance and develop innovative ways to deal with the potential negative effects of the intervention. Influence management to support and provide resources for the performance improvement intervention. Coordinate implementation efforts involving complex interventions that cross multiple business divisions. Coach and mentor others in the selection and implementation of interventions and in forecasting the effects of an intervention on the organization. Provide coaching on gaining management support and commitment of resources for interventions.

PROJECT MANAGEMENT. Plan, organize, and oversee implementation of interventions in complex business situations. Develop innovative ways to manage all aspects of the intervention including planning, resource management, communication, and tracking and measuring results outlined in the client contract. Coach and mentor others on developing project plans, managing people and resources, and communicating with clients and team members.

PERFORMANCE MEASUREMENT. Suggest to clients innovative approaches to using a balanced HPI scorecard of measures to determine the success of performance interventions. Assess the effectiveness of measurement strategies and evaluation tools and recommend improvements. Devise creative ways to remove barriers to the implementation of a performance scorecard. Coach and mentor others on selecting appropriate measurement initiatives. Provide coaching on developing measurement tools, implementing analysis techniques, and using evaluation data.

BUSINESS KNOWLEDGE. Assist clients in incorporating information about competitive and industry trends into their business plans. Create strategies to ensure that HPI interventions are aligned with the strategic direction of the organization and business division goals. Coach and mentor others on how to use competitive and industry knowledge in support of achieving organizational goals.

SYSTEMS THINKING. Assess the effectiveness of current systems that influence performance and business results within the organization. Work with clients to develop innovative approaches for aligning systems that support improved performance. Design approaches with client support to reengineer current processes and systems to support required performance. Coach and mentor others in identifying interrelationships among systems that affect organizational performance.

COACHING. Monitor the implementation of coaching and feedback by managers and make recommendations for improvement. Assess the capabilities and limitations of coaching tools and models and recommend innovative techniques to improve effectiveness. Coach and mentor others on methods, tools, and techniques in coaching team members.

COMMUNICATION. Implement creative approaches to obtaining information in ambiguous and complex business situations. Frame issues and potential solutions within the broader context of how they fit with the organizational strategy and business goals. Coach and mentor others on establishing a communication strategy, implementation plans, and organizational communication techniques.

PROBLEM SOLVING. For complex business situations, devise innovative ways of determining the gap between current and desired performance. Assess the degree to which root causes have been identified for organization-wide performance gaps and recommend methodologies for cause analysis. Assess and select creative approaches to problem solving. Coach and mentor others in how to define gaps between current and desired performance and how to identify root causes. Provide coaching on selecting and implementing appropriate courses of action.

Core Competencies/Job Functions—Leadership

FUNCTION AS A CHANGE AGENT. Work effectively with senior management offering fresh, practical approaches to solving complex business issues. Use knowledge of business, industry, and management to support building a realistic vision for the organization. Seek out and adapt best practices and manage change to achieve that vision.

PROVIDE EFFECTIVE LEADERSHIP. Demonstrate ethical standards. Establish a climate within the HPI department that fosters accountability, openness, trust, mutual respect, and ownership. Meet frequently with team members to provide feedback for improved performance. Recognize and reward improved performance, dedication, and excellence. Demonstrate the highest standards of personal and business integrity.

FOCUS ON ACTION AND RESULTS. Apply analysis, wisdom, experience, and judgment to make good decisions. Take personal accountability for making decisions. Seek the help and advice of others as needed. Accept and delegate tasks. Set clear objectives, deadlines, and measures. Monitor progress and results.

MAXIMIZE DIVERSITY. Create a supportive environment for all employees, demonstrating that fair and equal treatment of all team members is of highest priority.

DEMONSTRATE FLEXIBILITY AND PERSEVERANCE. Maintain flexibility despite conflicting demands in the work environment. Effectively balance work and personal priorities. Pursue responsibilities to closure, demonstrating energy and drive.

DEMONSTRATE SERVICE QUALITY EXCELLENCE. Display dedication in meeting and exceeding the expectations and requirements of service partners. Maintain effective relationships with service partners, gaining their trust and respect.

MANAGE THE DEPARTMENT EFFECTIVELY. Accept responsibility for hiring, managing, and developing a high-performing team. Prepare and manage a department budget with a business plan supporting organizational values and goals.

Education and Experience

EDUCATION. Master's degree required in education, business, or related discipline. Complete the performance consulting workshop and measurement workshop within 6 months of employment.

EXPERIENCE. Minimum of 12 years as a manager and senior consultant in organization development, quality, human resources, training, or related functions.

Selected List of HPI Associations

American Management Association (AMA)
1601 Broadway
New York, NY 10019
212.903.7935 Fax: 212.903.8168
www.amanet.org

American Society for Quality (ASQ)
P.O. Box 3005
Milwaukee, WI 53201
414.272.8575 Fax: 414.272.1734
www.asq.org

ASTD
1640 King Street, Box 1443
Alexandria, VA 22313
703.683.8100 Fax: 703.683.8103
www.astd.org

Association for Quality & Participation (AQP)
Executive Building, Suite 200
2368 Victory Parkway
Cincinnati, OH 45206
800.733.3310 513.381.1959 Fax: 513.381.0070
www.aqp.org

Human Resource Planning Society (HRPS)
317 Madison Avenue, Suite 1509
New York, NY 10017
212.490.6387 Fax: 212.682.6851
www.hrps.org

International Federation of Training & Development Organisations Ltd. (IFTDO)
1800 Duke Street
Alexandria, VA 22314
703.535.6011 Fax: 703.836.0367
www.iftdo.org

International Society for Performance Improvement (ISPI)
1300 L Street NW, Suite 1250
Washington, DC 20005
202.408.7969 Fax: 202.408.7972
www.ispi.org

Information Technology Training Association (ITTA)
8400 N. Mopac Expressway, Suite 201
Austin, TX 78759
512.502.9300, Ext. 201 Fax: 512.502.9308
www.itta.org

National Staff Development Council (NSDC)
PO Box 240
Oxford, OH 45056
513.523.6029 Fax: 513.523.0638
www.nsdc.org

Organization Development Network (ODN)
76 South Orange Avenue, Suite 101
South Orange, NJ 07079
973.763.7337 Fax: 973.763.7488
www.odnetwork.org

Professional Society for Sales & Marketing Training (SMT)
1900 Arch Street
Philadelphia, PA 19103
215.564.3484 Fax: 215.564.2175
www.smt.org

Society for Human Resources Management (SHRM)
1800 Duke Street
Alexandria, VA 22314
703.548.3440, Ext. 6108 Fax: 703.836.0367
www.shrm.org

Example of a University Model for a Decentralized Department

ABC University

Business Unit Executive — **Director, ABC University (HPI Leader)** — **Board of Regents—Chair**

CORPORATE COLLEGE TEAMS

- Business development and planning
- External relationships
- Administrative services
- Consulting services
- Relationship managers
- Cross-functional teams

Support internal sales and coordinate HPI products and services.

Coordinate needs for external providers.

Provide all administrative support to employees organization-wide.

Engage in performance consulting and leadership development.

Be assigned to key clients for needs assessment, communication, and coordination of HPI support.

Provide performance consulting interventions for organization-wide performance problems.

BUSINESS UNIT COLLEGES

The Business Unit Colleges provide products and services in support of business-specific goals and initiatives. The major areas of performance support provided to business include:

- Do performance consulting in partnership with line management to assess the root causes of poor performance, identify appropriate measures, agree on the causes and gaps, identify best practices to achieve expected performance, and plan actions to close the gap.
- Design and develop training solutions to help employees with the skills and knowledge needed to improve performance.
- Implement flexible delivery strategies based on business needs and employee learning styles.
- Measure the effectiveness of internal consulting and training initiatives in improving employee skills and knowledge, the impact of the application of those skills on the job, and improvement in operational and/or financial indicators.
- Team with the corporate colleges in supporting client business needs.

173

ABC University

Director, ABC University ——— **Board of Regents—Chair**
(HPI Leader)

CORPORATE COLLEGE: CONSULTING SERVICES TEAM

Performance Consulting

The Consulting Services Team provides services in diagnosing root causes of corporate-wide performance gaps, identifies work environment actions, HR actions, learning actions and client actions to improve business results, and provides a knowledge management database to leverage business opportunities.

- Create and maintain an online knowledge management process for capturing internal and external business best practices and leveraging knowledge into business opportunities.
- Provide project management and coordination for performance support of organization business unit.
- Partner with line management to identify and evaluate success measures (financial and operations) for performance support initiatives.
- Do internal consulting to improve shareholder value through organization improvement in turnover, prioritization processes, and identify systemic and individual productivity gains.
- Conduct workshops on performance consulting, quality tools, and measurement.
- Plan and coordinate mergers and acquisitions HPI support.

- Corporate-wide focus on improving results through:
  — Performance consulting
  — Process improvement (quality)
- Implementation support
- Sales and Service process support
- Measurement process
- Best practices/knowledge management database
- Merger and acquisitions management
- Leadership development
- All employee orientation
- Competency models, development planning

Leadership Development

The Consulting Services Team provides support for the education and training of first line supervisors, middle managers, and executives in the leadership skills needed to improve employee satisfaction and achieve ABC University's strategic goals.

- Implement a delivery strategy using high-tech tools (CBT, video conference, intranet) and high-touch (classroom) venues that meet the geographic and scheduling needs of organization's leaders.
- Identify outsourcing opportunities for leadership training.
- Create an executive development program with leading universities and organizations and implement internal discussion groups to share ideas on leveraging business opportunities.
- Support competency development and 360-degree assessments with external coaches for selected executives.
- Create a leadership development guide.
- Design, deliver, and continuously upgrade leadership development program for middle/first-line managers.
- Identify work-environment barriers to implementing quality leadership behaviors and the actions needed for improved employee satisfaction and productivity.
- Create and implement a mandatory introduction to organization values, history, lines of business, and immediate office products knowledge for all newly hired employees.

ABC University

Director, ABC University ——————————— **Board of Regents——Chair**
(HPI Leader)

CORPORATE COLLEGE: ADMINISTRATIVE SERVICES TEAM

The Team provides organization-wide administrative process and HPI technology services in support of the company's strategic direction, values, and goals.

- Administration services including
  - — core enrollment/scheduling
  - — data entry and reporting
  - — transcripts, catalog

- Research and development to leverage existing and future system capabilities to enhance employee learning and productivity

- CBT design and programming skills

- Intranet design and programming for online scheduling, registration, data reporting, referencing (development guides, catalog, etc.), communication

- Electronic performance support tools design and support

- Videoconference training design and delivery

- Learning centers to support employee development

ABC University

Director, ABC University ——————————————— **Board of Regents——Chair**
(HPI Leader)

CORPORATE COLLEGE: EXTERNAL PARTNERSHIP TEAM

The External Partnerships Team is responsible for coordinating the outsourcing and external support for all colleges of the University, providing coordination for internal and external programs for staff areas, and creating a general studies curriculum available to all employees.

- Coordinate the outsourcing of the general studies curriculum to colleges, organizations, and professional associations (ABA, AIB, etc.).

- Assist the staff areas in creating development guides for each job family.

- Coordinate with the other colleges in creating a supplier database on existing supplier relationships to avoid duplication, keep project status, and maintain a record of service quality.

- Coordinate executive performance consulting training and office products training for all employees.

ABC University

Director, University (HPI Leader) ———— **Board of Regents—Chair**

ABC UNIVERSITY BOARD OF REGENTS

ROLE: To provide strategic direction, focus, and priorities in support of University initiatives.

Meeting:
- Quarterly

Member
- Chairman or CEO
- Business unit executives
- Staff executives
- Secretary—Director of ABC University

Duties
- Support the vision and values of the organization as the foundation for all College products and services.
- Coordinate and reconcile organization-wide business imperatives and business unit goals with University initiatives.
- Create a charter that clearly establishes the role, accountabilities, and minimum standards of performance expected by the Board of Regents and college advisory boards.
- Establish priorities for University initiatives and resources that support the organization's strategic direction.
- Review the University's qualitative and operational/financial effect on the organization.
- Support the University as a change agent in improving employee satisfaction through effective implementation performance and process improvement initiatives.
- Take ownership for the products, services, and results achieved by ABC University.

177

ABC University

Director, University ——————————————————— **Board of Regents—Chair**
(HPI Leader)

UNIVERSITY COLLEGE ADVISORY BOARDS

ROLE: To provide strategic direction, focus, and priorities in support of business unit specific initiatives.

Member

Business Unit Colleges
- Chairman–Business Unit Executive
- Business Segment Executives
- Secretary-College HPI Manager

Meeting:
- At least quarterly

Duties

- Support the vision and values of the organization as the foundation for all College products and services.
- Coordinate and reconcile competing demands and recommend College priorities to support the business and organization's strategic direction.
- Create a charter that clearly establishes the role, accountabilities, and minimum standards of performance expected by the College and Advisory Board.
- Review the College's qualitative and operational/financial impact on the business and the organization.
- Support the University as a change agent in improving employee satisfaction through effective performance and process improvement initiatives.
- Take ownership for the products, services, and results achieved by the College.

References

Argyris, C. (1993). *Knowledge for Action: A Guide to Overcoming Barriers to Organizational Change*. San Francisco: Jossey-Bass.

ASTD. (1992). *Trainer's Toolkit: Evaluating Results of Training*. Alexandria, VA: Author.

Cummins, T.G., and Worley, C.G. (1998). *Organization Development and Change* (6th edition). Cincinnati: South-Western College Publishing.

Deming, W.E. (1988). *Out of the Crisis*. Cambridge, MA: MIT Center for Advanced Engineering Study.

Dick, W., and Carey, L. (1996). *The Systematic Design of Instruction* (4th edition). Glenview, IL: HarperCollins College Publishers.

Geis, G.L. (1986). "Human Performance Technology: An Overview." In *Introduction to Performance Technology* (volume 1), M.E. Smith, editor. Silver Spring, MD: International Society for Performance Improvement.

Gilbert, T.F. (1996). *Human Competence: Engineering Worthy Performance*. Silver Spring, MD: International Society for Performance Improvement.

Guba, E.G. (1989). *Fourth Generation Evaluation*. London: Sage Publications.

Handshaw, G.D., and LaBonte, T.J., and Robinson, J.C. (1998). *An Integrated Model for Human Performance Improvement*. International Society for Performance Improvement Annual Conference presentation.

Harless, J.H. (1975). *An Ounce of Analysis (Is Worth a Pound of Objectives)*. Newnan, GA: Harless Performance Guild.

Harless, J.H. (1994). *Accomplishment-Based Curriculum Development System*. Newnan, GA: Harless Performance Guild.

International Society for Performance Improvement. (1988). *Human Performance Technology Model*. Silver Spring, MD: Author.

Kaplan, R.S., and Norton, D.P. (1996). *The Balanced Scorecard: Translating Strategy Into Action*. Cambridge, MA: Harvard Business School Press.

Kaufman, R., editor. (1996). *Guidebook for Performance Improvement: Working With Individuals and Organizations*. San Francisco: Jossey-Bass.

Kirkpatrick, D.J. (1994). *Evaluating Training Programs: The Four Levels*. San Francisco: Berrett-Koehler Publishers.

LaBonte, T.J., and Robinson, J.C. (1999, August). "Performance Consulting: One Organization, One Human Performance Improvement Process." *Training & Development*, 32–37.

Mager, R.F., and Pipe, P. (1997). *Analyzing Performance Problems: Or You Really Oughta Wanna*. Atlanta: Center for Effective Performance.

National Institute of Standards and Technology. (1987). *The United States Malcolm Baldridge National Quality Award.* Washington, DC: U.S. Department of Commerce.

Phillips, J. (1997). *Handbook of Training Evaluation and Measurement Me*thods. Houston: Gulf Publishing.

Robinson, D.G., and Robinson, J.C. (1995). *Performance Consulting: Moving Beyond Training.* San Francisco: Berrett-Koehler Publishers.

Robinson, D.G., and Robinson, J.C., editors. (1998). *Moving From Training to Performance: A Practical Guidebook.* Alexandria, VA: ASTD.

Rummler, G.A., and Brache, A.P. (1995). *Improving Performance: How to Manage the White Space on the Organization Chart* (2d edition). San Francisco: Jossey-Bass.

Skinner, B.F. (1953). *Beyond Freedom and Dignity.* New York: Random House.

Stake, R.E. (1991). *Advances in Program Evaluation: Effects of Changes in Assessment Policy.* Stamford, CT: JAI Press.

Stolovitch, H.D., and Keeps, E.J., editors. (1999). *Handbook of Human Performance Technology: A Comprehensive Guide for Analyzing and Solving Performance Problems in Organizations* (2d edition). San Francisco: Jossey-Bass.

Stufflebeam, D.L. (1988). *Systematic Evaluation: A Self-Instructional Guide to Theory and Practice.* Thousand Oaks, CA: Corwin Press.

Ulrich, D. (1998, January–February). "A New Mandate for Human Resources." *Harvard Business Review,* 124–134.

Wile, D. (1996). "Why Doers Do." *Performance and Improvement Journal, 35*(2): 30–35.

Further Resources

Biech, E. (1999). *The Business of Consulting: The Basics and Beyond*. San Francisco: Jossey-Bass.

Block, P. (1999). *Flawless Consulting: A Guide to Getting Your Expertise Used* (2d edition). San Francisco: Jossey-Bass.

Bricker, B. (1992). "Basics of Performance Technology." *Info-line*, issue no. 9211. Alexandria, VA: ASTD.

Callahan, M. (1998). "The Role of the Performance Evaluator." *Info-line*, issue no. 9803. Alexandria, VA: ASTD.

Chang, R.Y., and DeYoung, P. (1996). *Measuring Organizational Improvement Impact: A Practical Guide to Successfully Linking Organizational Improvement Measures*. Irvine, CA: Richard Chang Associates.

Chang, R.Y., and Morgan, M.W. (2000). *Performance Scorecards: Measuring the Right Things in the Real World*. San Francisco: Jossey-Bass.

Dean, P., and Ripley, D., editors. (1997). *Performance Improvement Pathfinders: Models for Organizational Learning Systems*. Silver Spring, MD: International Society for Performance Improvement.

Drucker, P.F. (1964). *Managing for Results*. New York: Harper and Row.

Fuller, J., and Sugrue, B., editors. (1999). *Performance Interventions: Selecting, Implementing, and Evaluating Results*. Alexandria, VA: ASTD.

Gilley, J.W., and Goffern, A.J. (1993). *The Role of the Internal Consultant*. Burr Ridge, IL: Irwin Professional Publishing.

Hale, J.A. (1998). *The Performance Consultant's Fieldbook: Tools and Techniques for Improving Organizations and People*. San Francisco: Pfeiffer.

Harless, J.H. (1995). "Performance Technology Skills in Business: Implications for Preparation." *Performance Improvement Quarterly*, 8(4).

Holdaway, K., and Saunders, M. (1992). *The In-House Trainer as Consultant*. San Diego: Pfeiffer.

Holloway, J., editor. (1995). *Performance Measurement and Evaluation*. Thousand Oaks, CA: Sage Publications.

Kaydos, W. (1991). *Measuring, Managing, and Maximizing Performance: What Every Manager Needs to Know About Quality and Productivity to Make Real Improvements in Performance*. Portland, OR: Productivity Press.

Koehle, D. (1997). "The Role of the Performance Change Manager." *Info-line*, issue no. 9715. Alexandria, VA: ASTD.

Maslow, A.H. (1954). *Motivation and Personality*. New York: Harper and Row.

Rothwell, W.J., Sanders, E.S., and Soper, J.G. (1999). *ASTD Models for Workplace Learning and Performance: Roles, Competencies, and Outputs.* Alexandria, VA: ASTD.

Senge, P.M. (1990). *The Fifth Discipline.* New York: Doubleday.

Skinner, B.F. (1978). *Reflections on Behaviorism and Society.* Upper Saddle River, NJ: Prentice Hall.

Society for Human Resources Management Foundation. (1997). *The Competency Initiative: Standards of Excellence for Human Resources Executives.* Alexandria, VA: Author.

Swanson, R.A. (1994). *Analysis for Improving Performance: Tools for Diagnosing Organizations and Documenting Workplace Expertise.* San Francisco: Berrett-Koehler.

Ulrich, D. (1997). *Human Resource Champions: The Next Agenda for Adding Value and Delivering Results.* Cambridge, MA: Harvard Business School Press.

Watson, G.H. (1993). *The Benchmarking Workbook: Adapting Best Practices for Performance Improvement.* Portland, OR: Productivity Press.

About the Author

Tom LaBonte is a human performance improvement professional with experience as a training director and HR director in business, government, and academia. As the consulting services director at Ulysses Learning, Tom is responsible for implementing judgment and skills e-learning solutions and getting results. He has previously held the positions of HR executive with Centura Banks and senior vice president of performance improvement and training at PNC Bank. Tom collaborated with Jim Robinson on an article for the August 1999 edition of *Training & Development* entitled "Performance Consulting, One Process, One Team" and wrote a chapter for the book *Moving From Training to Performance: A Practical Guidebook,* edited by Dana and Jim Robinson. Tom is a frequent speaker on performance consulting, HR and learning strategies, and organization development at national conferences. Tom served on the ASTD board from 1998 to 2000 and currently serves on the ASTD national nominating committee. He also serves the ISPI Carolinas chapter, and the Mecklenburg Area Council of the Boy Scouts of America. Tom earned undergraduate and graduate degrees at the University of Maryland at College Park. Tom and his wife live in Charlotte, North Carolina, and enjoy travel and ancient and medieval history. He may be reached via email at tjlabonte@earthlink.net.